WORLD WAR II
BUFFALO

WORLD WAR II BUFFALO

Gretchen E. Knapp

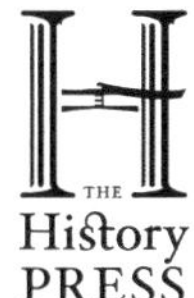

Published by The History Press
Charleston, SC
www.historypress.net

First published 2017

Manufactured in the United States

ISBN 9781467136952

Library of Congress Control Number: 2017948513

Notice: The information in this book is true and complete to the best of our knowledge. It is offered without guarantee on the part of the author or The History Press. The author and The History Press disclaim all liability in connection with the use of this book.

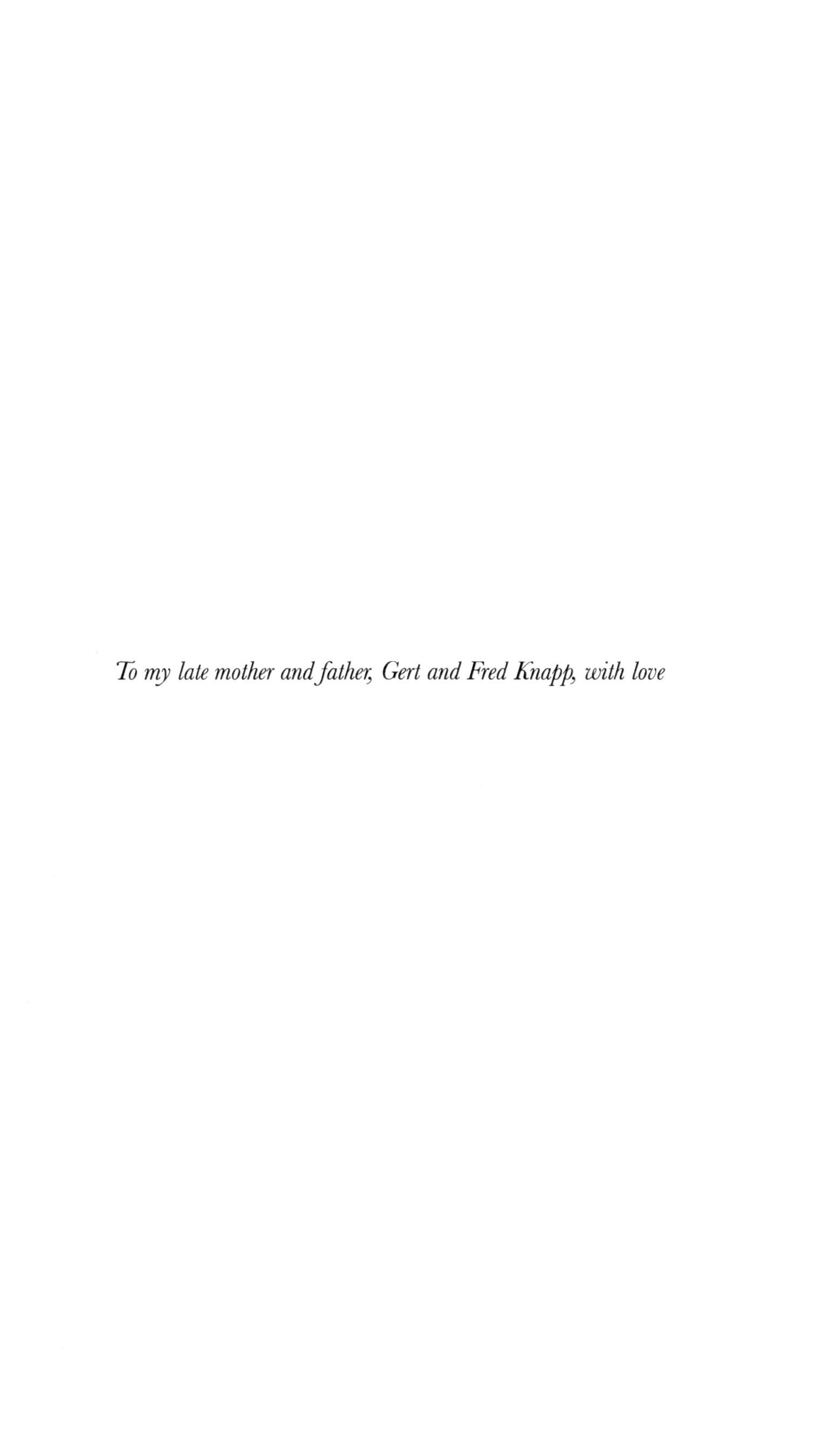

To my late mother and father, Gert and Fred Knapp, with love

CONTENTS

ACKNOWLEDGEMENTS

Many thanks are owed to the archivists and librarians of the National Archives and Records Administration (William Creech and Richard Boylan), Library of Congress Manuscript Division, New York State Archives (Daniel Linke and William Gorman), New York State Library, University at Buffalo Archives (William Offhaus), Buffalo State University Archives, Buffalo History Museum (Cynthia Van Ness), Buffalo and Erie County Public Library (William Loos), Canisius College Archives, Fort Niagara, Niagara Falls Public Library (Don Loker), Historical Society of the Tonawandas (Ned Schimminger and Skip Johnson), International Institute of Buffalo, Immigration History Research Center and Social Welfare History Archives (University of Minnesota), National Board of the Young Women's Christian Association, New York State Military Museum, Sisters of St. Francis at Stella Niagara (Mary Serbacki, OSF), the Minerva Center, Young Men's Christian Association and the United States Holocaust History Museum.

The interlibrary loan wizards at the University at Buffalo, Eastern Illinois University and Illinois State University deserve high praise.

I am greatly indebted to the late Dr. Karl Hartzell, the New York state historian whose conscientious collecting of documents and photographs during World War II made this work possible.

Thank you very much to Rosemary Dold, Marianne Ferber, Emanuel "Manny" Fried, Jay Garner, Paula Kaleta, Carol Pujolas, Karen Simpson and Joan Busch Staley for sharing their remembrances and pointing me to more information. Thomas Bolze, Kate Butler, Megan Cavitt, Mary Clare

Dolata, Amber Finck, Paula Kaleta, Ann Marie Przybyl, Michele Raupp, Crystal Robinson, Leo Schpilkes, Paula Wager and Vicki Walsh contributed valuable suggestions and unflagging support. I am most appreciative to Margaret Abels (Nardin Academy), Judy Einach, Timothy McCarthy (Nichols School), the Pujolas family and Carol Schmeidler for sharing their private collections.

To my husband, Angelo Capparella, who encouraged me throughout the creative process, thank you for applying a keen eye to my work and practicing endless patience.

INTRODUCTION

Under a grassy rise in Elmlawn Cemetery next to my paternal family's plot lies Private First Class Francis N. Dempfle, U.S. Army. He died on December 13, 1944, at age twenty-one. His was the first burial in the Field of Honor.

Once a month, Mom, Dad and I put flowers on my grandparents' grave and gave a respectful nod to Great-Aunt Ella. I wandered to look at Private Dempfle's grave, as I always did.

"He died during the war," said my father, putting his hand on my shoulder. I was nine, and the only war I knew was in Vietnam, where my cousin served. "We spoke with his family once. Very sad."

Dempfle enlisted in Buffalo on February 12, 1943. He was a member of the 2nd Platoon, Company K, 311th Infantry, 78th Division, known as the "Lightning Division." The 78th landed in France ready for combat on November 22, 1944, and entered the Hurtgen forest in Germany on December 10. Three days later, Dempfle was dead.

James Cooper's father served with Francis. "On the day he disappeared, Francis was making his way back to the company command post from an engagement in the forest. He never made it back, and no one knew what had happened to him."

Later, I discovered that the Hurtgen forest battles were among the deadliest and most senseless during the war in Europe. His remains were discovered in Germany in 1976 and returned to the United States for burial near Buffalo. The Germans erected a monument in the forest to mark the location where he and three other missing soldiers were found. The Department of War awarded him the Purple Heart and the Bronze Star Medal.

Until 1976, I was visiting an empty grave.

I knew my father enlisted in the U.S. Navy days after the Japanese attacked Pearl Harbor, Hawaii, on December 7, 1941. So did his best friend, Bruce Stark, and my uncle Edward McCarthy. Uncle Arnold Dold served in the U.S. Army in Germany during the war and later in its occupation. Aunt Rose flew a plane that she co-owned with other women pilots in the Civil Air Patrol. My mother and her sister Geraldine and their friends and relatives worked at Curtiss-Wright. Every male neighbor, teacher or family friend of a certain age was a veteran. (I didn't meet a female veteran until 1992.) They were everyday Americans who had done extraordinary things.

That was the first reason I became interested in World War II.

My parents celebrated their twenty-fifth wedding anniversary when I was twelve. They took me along to Hawaii to visit Pearl Harbor, where my father had been posted, serving on aircraft bound for Midway. Hotels had replaced command posts, but the outline of the war's impact was visible through my father's eyes. We visited the newly built USS *Arizona* memorial, the final resting place for the ship's 1,177 crewmen, who lost their lives due to the surprise Japanese attack. The pale flower wreaths bobbed in the waters on each side of the long white structure in memory of the fallen.

And that was the second reason for my interest in the war.

In 2011, I was cleaning out my childhood home after my parents passed away and found the red laundry washboard that had served as a mirror in the back hall. In gold letters, the date "July 31, 1943," was painted across the top. It was the day that they were married.

I half-remembered the story. Every weekday, my mother took the streetcar from Thompson Street to work at Farrell-Birmingham, a defense plant that manufactured gears for the navy. Before my father, a navy aviation machinist's mate first class, shipped out to the Pacific, he sent for her. In my mind, I see her looking around in amazement at the bustling crowds in the Central Terminal, clutching a small suitcase that held her handmade wedding suit. I can only imagine the fortitude needed for a young woman who had never been outside Buffalo to endure the long train ride to the naval base in Jacksonville, Florida.

President Roosevelt's own chaplain, an Episcopal priest, performed the wedding service. A married couple my father knew stood up for them in the base's little chapel. After a brief honeymoon in St. Augustine, where Ponce de Leon allegedly discovered the Fountain of Youth, both drank from

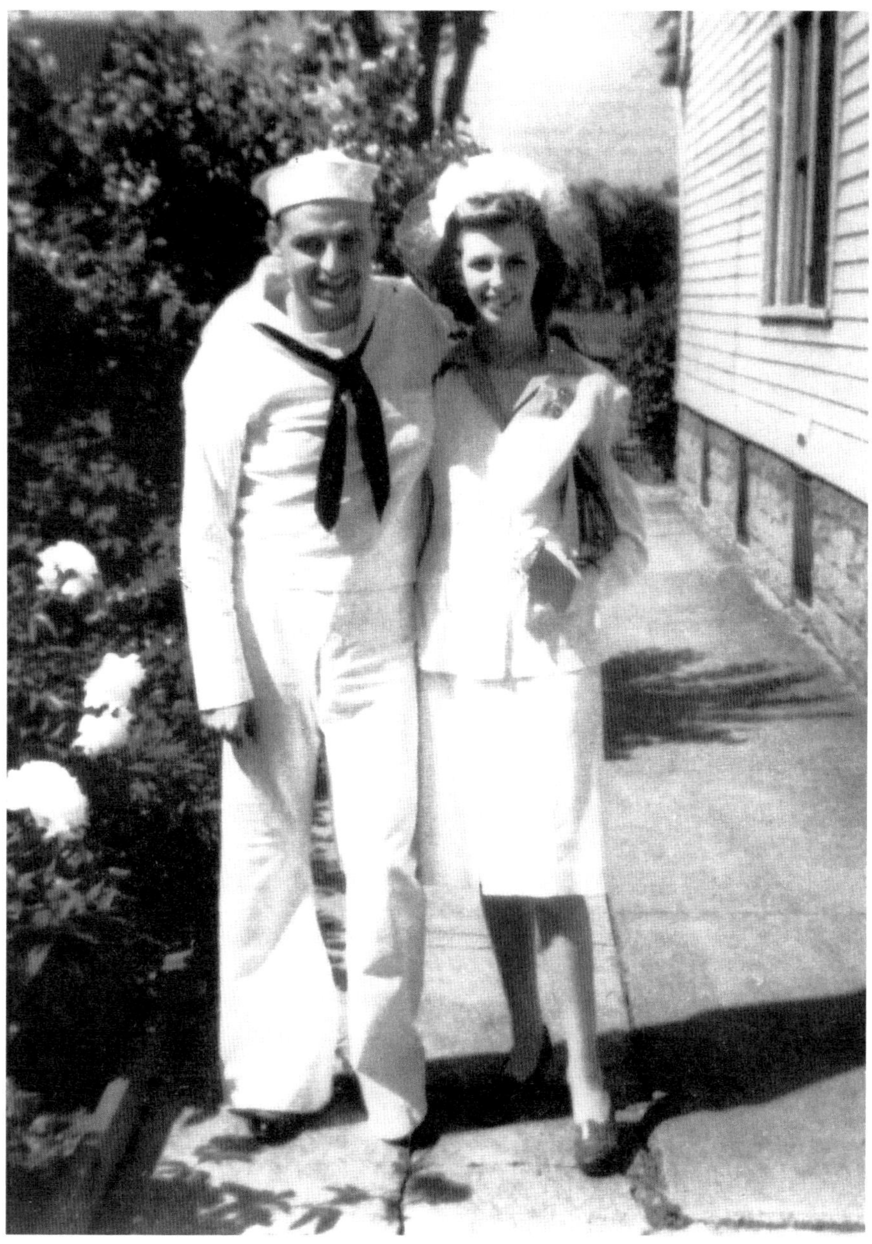

Wedding of Frederick and Gertrude Knapp, Jacksonville, Florida Naval Base, 1943.
Author's collection.

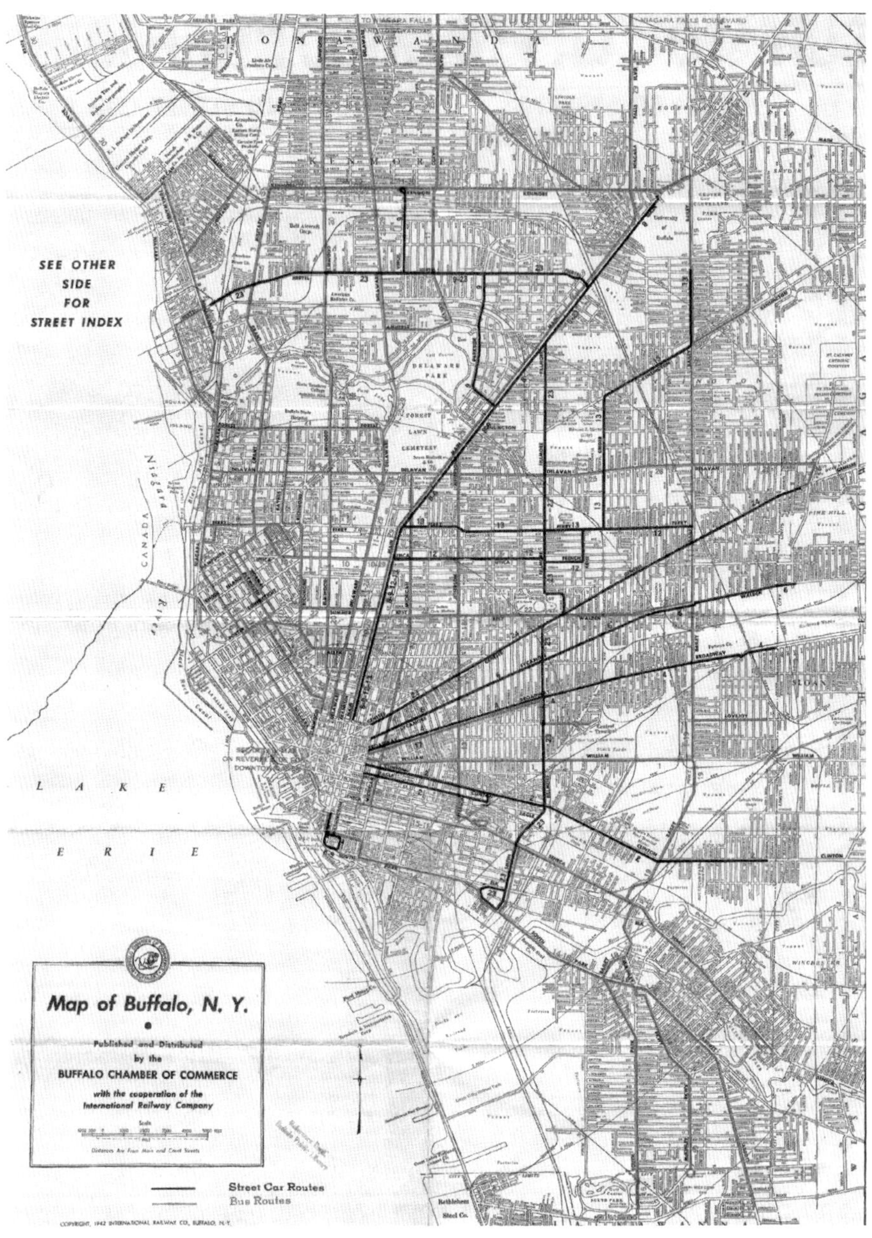

Map of Buffalo, 1942. *Reproduction by permission of the Buffalo & Erie County Public Library, Buffalo, New York.*

a battered tin cup. Mom returned to Buffalo to work as a salvage manager at Curtiss-Wright. Dad came back after three years and ten months to attend college in Oswego, thanks to the G.I. Bill. The old-fashioned red laundry washboard now resides in my house.

And that was the final nudge to write about the war.

But why Buffalo? That's easy. My parents were from Black Rock and attended Riverside High School and Buffalo State College, then known as State Teachers College. Most of my relatives live here. I grew up in the town of Tonawanda, attended Kenmore East High School and graduated from the University at Buffalo.

My ancestors were immigrants who left Germany in the mid-1880s to make the long and perilous journey across the Atlantic. They made Buffalo their home, as did countless newcomers from Great Britain, France, Ireland, Italy, Poland and the Ukraine. Wherever I reside, Buffalo will always be home.

In this book, the people and events of World War II's homefront take center stage. The history of land and sea battles, strategies and tactics are best read elsewhere.

Scores of books have been published on the reasons for World War II. My explanation is simplistic, given the size of this work. World War II began when a dictator, Adolf Hitler, came to power in Germany in 1933. He and his followers, including paramilitary groups, inflamed hatred against Jews (and others) and passed laws that made life impossible for them to remain in the country. Great Britain tried to appease Hitler by permitting Germany to annex Czechoslovakia in 1938, and then Germany invaded Austria and Poland in 1939 and other nations in quick succession. Fascist leader Mussolini arose in Italy. Meanwhile, Hitler's hatred of the Jews led to the "Final Solution": the genocide of an entire people. The remaining free European powers and Great Britain (the Allies) declared war on Germany in 1939, but the United States didn't want to intervene, preferring isolation. Japan's surprise attack on American territory in Hawaii led to the immediate declaration of war against Japan and entrance into the war in Europe. (For a much clearer description of the war's beginnings and course, examine the bibliography.)

For Buffalo, the war began in 1940 due to an obscure piece of legislation that tapped into the area's factories and skilled workforce. The Lend-Lease Act propelled the defense industry into manufacturing ships, aircraft, ordnance and artillery for the Allied nations. Food—grown and processed on American soil—and oil were provided without payment. In return, the

United States used army and naval bases in Allied lands as staging areas during the war.

Western New York began fulfilling defense needs one year before the Japanese attacked Hawaii. The city of Buffalo, wrote a journalist for the *New York Times*, was "like a mining town that had just struck gold."

1

WINDS OF CHANGE

He's coming," said Mayor Thomas Holling to the waiting crowd assembling at 10:00 a.m. on an overcast November morning. A murmur of excitement ran through the crowd gathered in Niagara Square, many on their lunch hour. Fifteen minutes later, the mayor lifted his arms to quiet the milling throng and said again, "He's leaving the Curtiss-Wright plant." Another fifteen minutes went by, and the mayor shouted, "Any minute now!" After two more promises, Holling said, "Well, at least in a couple of minutes," and the crowd of thirty thousand cheered. The Erie County Democratic Drill Team gave out miniature American flags, and a drum corps played patriotic music.

Then the sirens shrieked, and President Franklin Delano Roosevelt waved from the motorcade that threaded through the streets toward Niagara Square and city hall. The day was Friday, November 1, 1940.

"Today, it is my supreme privilege," Mayor L. Holling said, "as the mayor of Buffalo, the city of good neighbors, Mr. President, to again extend to you our heartfelt greetings and our best wishes for your success." President Roosevelt toured the Curtiss-Wright plant for half an hour, with the workers saluting him, then traveled to the Bell plant on Elmwood Avenue, where he was met by plant owner Larry Bell, to inspect eight P-39 Airacobras. These innovative American fighter aircraft were popular among the British, Canadian, Free French, Italian and Army Air Corps.

At the president's arrival, the aviation employees spontaneously moved into precise production model, each man perfectly completing his task.

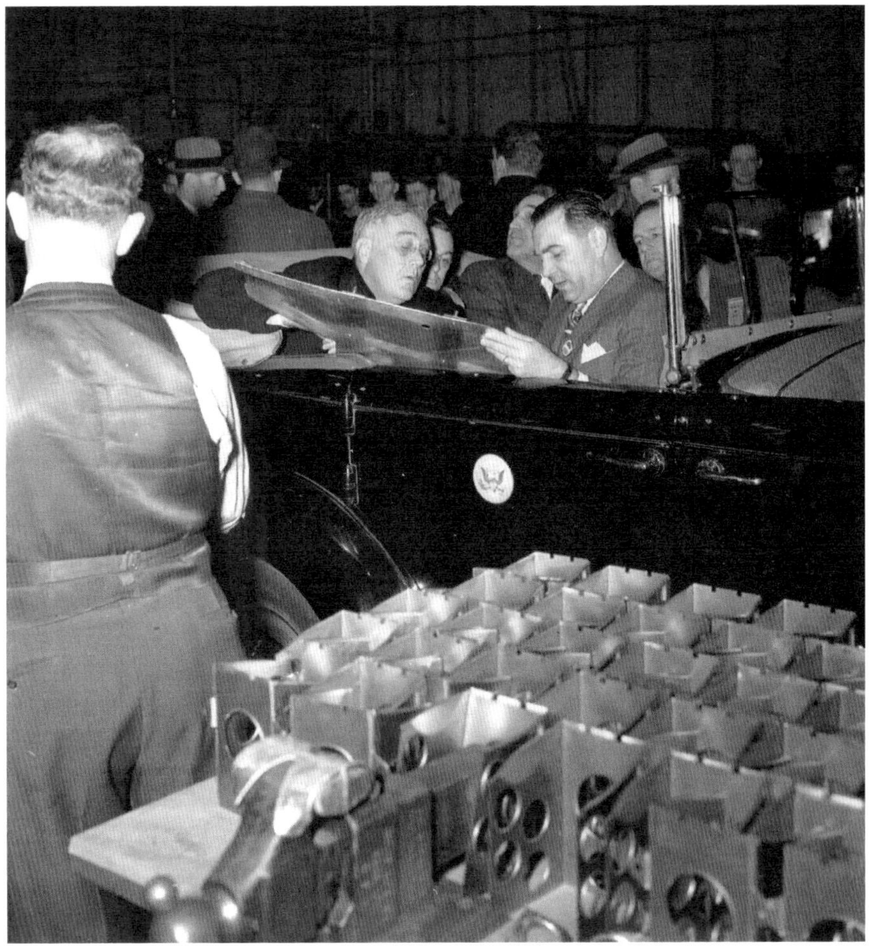

President Franklin D. Roosevelt and Lawrence Bell touring the Bell plant in 1940. *Courtesy of the Buffalo History Museum, used by permission.*

Roosevelt said, "I can't see you all in the shops, but I have been through them and I am very much thrilled by what I have seen." His motorcade, accompanied by officials walking to either side, drove through the half-mile-long plant.

As the motorcade came down Broadway to Fillmore, the East Side crowds jammed the sidewalks, and from there the caravan traveled to Lackawanna, where Roosevelt visited Bethlehem Steel.

Back at the steps of city hall, a striking art deco building, President Roosevelt said, "I have been inspecting some plants this morning, plants which are turning out airplanes. The world today is going through the kind of a storm that we hope will soon be over." He paused, looking over the podium at the crowd. "I hope and I believe that this administration will be able to keep this country at peace during the next four years." Winding up his campaign speech, Roosevelt said, "I ask and I think I will get your help in that."

The *Buffalo Courier-Express*, one of two city newspapers, carried a headline that supported presidential candidate Wendell Willkie instead of covering the visit of the leading Democrat in the United States. Willkie, the Republican, railed against Roosevelt for the nation's inadequate military preparedness. But Roosevelt preempted Willkie's criticism by establishing the first peacetime conscription and ordering defense contracts to supply the Allies.

The procession of twenty cars left the square and returned to the specially established train crossing where the American Legion Post No. 20 of Blasdell turned out with a color guard of honor. The president waved his hat in thanks and said goodbye. The train whistled, and off he went.

Buffalo's war council began under Mayor Holling, a Democrat, whose term ended in 1940. His successor, Mayor Kelly, also a Democrat, appointed his own people for key positions. Former New York Supreme Court justice Daniel Kennefick was named the chair of the council. The remainder of the twenty-two members included the superintendent of schools, public works,

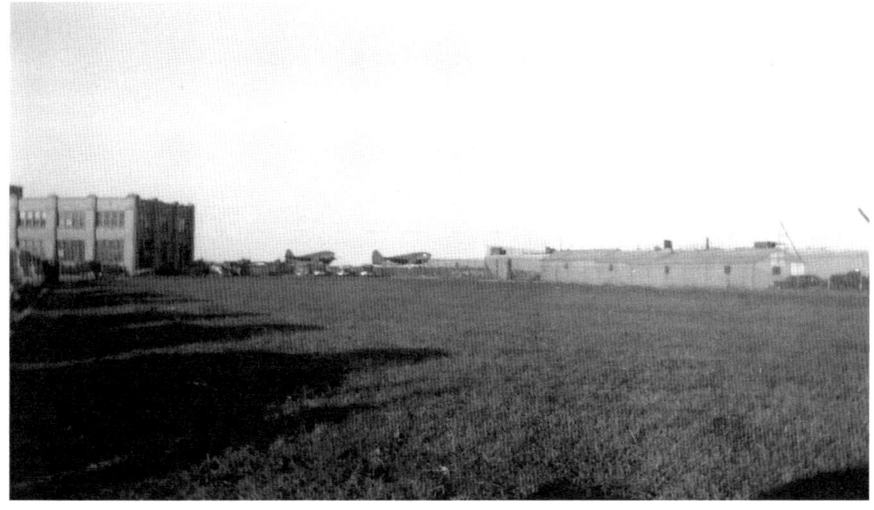

Curtiss-Wright airfield. *Author's collection.*

fire and police, the comptroller and local businessmen. The council was a bureaucratic nightmare with fifteen major committees, each of which had subcommittees. Most of the work was handled by a seven-member executive committee, which met weekly. Erie County, Niagara County, Lackawanna, the City of Tonawanda, North Tonawanda, the Town of Tonawanda, Lockport and Niagara Falls each had their own war council.

Territorial disputes were common. One federal mandate encouraged staggered hours for retailers and offices to reduce pressure on the streetcars and buses. Buffalo and Erie Counties set up war transportation committees. But the Erie County War Council resisted the Buffalo plan because of long-standing resentment of Buffalo's domineering influence over county matters. The Erie War Council included members of AFL and CIO labor unions; the Buffalo War Council did not. Despite numerous hearings, organized labor groups supported the county's refusal to accept Buffalo's staggered hours plan although the transportation shortage had reached crisis levels.

Buffalo's council then had to grant exemptions to large employers in the city from its own staggered hours plan because they were competing with county plants opening one half hour earlier. After several hearings in Albany and Buffalo, both the Bell and Curtiss-Wright plants accepted the city's plan. The council had no choice but to agree, but most significant was participation of organized labor on the Buffalo War Council, including the CIO representative, who had been characterized as "a bag of wind." Council committees and subcommittees studied social problems as temporary obstacles to fulfilling production quotas and not as long-standing difficulties. Social workers shared studies prepared by the chamber of commerce. Women on the council were limited to volunteer coordination, nursing and nutrition. Blacks, Jews and Italians were not offered membership.

The Buffalo War Council's bias toward business and commerce meant that the key position of executive secretary was given to Dudley M. Irwin Jr., with a two-year leave of absence from his partnership in a local stock exchange firm. His superior, Mr. Schoellkopf, sat on the Niagara Falls War Council. Remington Rand, a large manufacturer, provided Irwin with an assistant as the workload increased.

The Buffalo Council formed a small "nationality groups and civil liberties" committee under a local attorney. But the interest in this committee was limited to discrimination against Italian Americans, although African Americans, women and members of other groups protested in vain to the War Council. The National Urban League and the International Institute were frustrated. These organizations appealed to the state, and the Buffalo

Committee on Discrimination in Employment would take up their cause in coming years.

Half of Buffalo's population was described as "native whites of American-born parentage," according to the 1940 U.S. Census. The remaining population was led by first- and second-generation Polish, Scots-Irish, German and Italian residents, and most western and eastern European, Middle Eastern and Spanish-speaking groups. The African American population was tiny. W.N. Kessel, manager of the chamber of commerce's Statistical and Research Division, referred to the city as a little League of Nations. Today's reference would be the United Nations.

In June 1941, President Roosevelt issued an executive order that reinforced the policy of nondiscrimination in the defense industry and established the Fair Employment Practices Committee. New York State formed a Committee on Discrimination in Employment through the New York State War Council in March 1941. By September 1941, federal and state legislation prohibited discrimination by race, creed or color at plants or other institutions engaged in war work. This included public utilities, public services and labor unions. In 1940, the state forbade discrimination in labor unions, civil service appointments, public housing and public work projects.

The state made violation of the statute a penal offense and sent field agents around the state. They persuaded defense contractors to comply, and to survey the hiring practices of 250 war plants to help defense industries secure the best workers. They had direct contacts with the War Department about employing aliens (i.e., undocumented immigrants) who were from Allied nations and consulted with businesses on the best ways to introduce minority workers into factories, carry out a comprehensive education program in the schools, labor and industry and distribute pamphlets.

In early October 1941, an enraged Italian American contractor murdered a New York City labor leader, claiming he discriminated against Italian Americans. Around the state, defense factory owners were alarmed. The city of Buffalo responded with the creation of an anti-discrimination committee organized under Judge Charles B. Sears, the state supreme court justice. (The University at Buffalo's law library is named after him.) Sears's influence in state politics and his long-standing interest in discrimination issues made him the best choice. Sears was president of the International Institute of Buffalo's board of directors. He was reluctant to become chair, but the governor himself intervened.

The judge appointed social worker Victor Einach as executive secretary of the Buffalo Committee on Discrimination in Employment. Einach was a western New York native educated at the then private University of Buffalo. He was on leave from his position as assistant executive secretary of the Buffalo Council of Social Agencies, which operated as a clearinghouse for all community social welfare services to prevent duplication. Educated at the University of Buffalo's new School of Social Work, Einach represented the new breed of social worker—a certified professional from an accredited school. He worked for the National Youth Authority, which helped young people during the Great Depression become employed, and produced a book in early 1941 titled *Channels of Defense*. This compilation listed and described the variety of defense programs open to the public. Until the end of 1943, he was also the committee's only staff member.

To broaden his knowledge of current concerns, Einach joined the Junior Chamber of Commerce, also known as the Jaycees; the International Institute; the Federal Council of Churches; the National Conference of Christians and Jews; and others. At the end of December 1942, the committee opened an office in downtown Buffalo and encouraged people who thought they had been discriminated against in defense employment to file complaints.

Even with Einach as the sole staff member, the committee handled 270 complaints in his first year. Two-thirds of the complaints came from blacks. The rest were filed by Italian Americans, Jews and undocumented immigrants. Half of the alleged discrimination occurred against women, mostly black women. Grievances were also registered by Ukrainian Americans and Seventh-day Adventists. The latter had religious reasons for not being able to work on Saturdays. To investigate these claims, Einach contacted local firms with defense contracts. Sometimes the state instigated the investigations. Later, during the war, the Buffalo Committee initiated contact for both educational and preventative purposes. One of Einach's cases involved the subject of a FBI investigation. Army Air Force workers circulated different anti-Semitic "poems" at Curtiss-Wright and Bell Aircraft in mid-1943. Local taverns gave them out, too. Here's one of the milder examples:

From the shore of Coney Island
Looking eastward to the Sea,
Stands a Kosher Air Raid Warden
Wearing "V" for Victory;
And as the breezes fill the air
From the "Dogs" at Nathan's stand,

Only Christian Boys are drafted
From Coney Island's sands.

Oh, we Jews are not afraid to say
We'll stay home and give first aid;
Let the Christian saps go fight the Japs
In the uniforms we made.
When the Army and the Navy
Draw near to battle scenes,
They will find the Jews
Selling boots and shoes
To United States Marines.

The FBI charged the offenders, and the handouts stopped.

As defense workers went through on-the-job training, they found better-paying jobs for their new skills. The biggest problem that the defense plants now had was piracy. As defense plants continued to induce steelworkers to change jobs, an earlier agreement signed by sixty war plants that employed eighty-six thousand people had not ended this problem. The federal government came up with a controlled referral plan as an experiment—it was called the "Buffalo Plan"—with the expectation that the plan would stop piracy in other cities, too. Anyone who was already registered through the U.S. Employment Service (USES), which was a requirement to land a defense job, was sent to high-priority war industry jobs. Every defense plant had drawn up a priority list, and each week the USES reviewed the list to determine which of the one hundred plants on the list should be rated either an *A* or a *B*, depending on how essential the product of these plants was to defense needs. If the war plants had not made the greatest possible use of all available workers, including women, they weren't on either list and would not get the workers they needed. This meant they would not be able to make their deadlines to finish products on time.

Labor unions endorsed the plan, but company representatives opposed it—although for the first time the factories made production goals. The chamber of commerce resisted the Buffalo Plan because members thought this would impede commerce. Over 40,000 male workers were referred in the first three months of the plan, which handled between 400 and 1,300 persons each day. Only 10 percent of the referrals were people looking to switch to another war job. The controlled referral plan did not stop piracy as planned but did severely reduce the problem. The plant that lost the worker had to replace that person, and this change encouraged the employment of women. By the end of September 1943, western New York topped all other New York communities in the percentage of women employed in defense plants, which were mainly the two aircraft giants: Curtiss-Wright and Bell Aircraft.

The plan also encouraged men to leave light industry for women workers and take up heavy industry positions because the iron and steel factories were completing only half of their contracts. After three steel furnaces shut down due to insufficient workers, ads to this end appealed to men:

> *Are you a tough guy? Have you got real red fighting blood in your veins? Then here is your chance to do vitally needed jobs in heavy war industry—a job that calls for a real two-fisted he-man! A job no woman can do: the kind of work you wouldn't want your sister or wife to do.*

The reason male workers were reluctant to take heavy industry positions was simple economics. The hourly wage scale of heavy industry was the highest among war industries in 1940 but did not offer the best pay rate during the war. Aircraft workers received one-third more in their paychecks than steelworkers, and to add insult to injury, the War Labor Board froze wages at these rates rather than equalizing them. The difference in pay between light and heavy industries was also found in the number of hours worked. Heavy industry employees worked over forty hours per week, while their counterparts in light war production worked a forty-eight-hour week. Since workers were paid by the hour, the difference in wages was significant.

Residents who had lived through the First World War (aka, the Great War) had feelings of déjà vu and fear of the "boom-bust" cycle the war had brought. Over twenty thousand persons left western New York for the armed forces in 1917. (America was reluctant to enter the war in Europe until it was almost over.) Numerous strikes over the wages and hours, the severe reduction in immigration and anti-German sentiments disrupted the homefront. Undeterred by labor problems, factory owners recruited groups previously banned from certain industrial positions, including African Americans and women. Employers utilized the newly established New York State employment service to find qualified workers with appropriate technical skills. Using advertisements, leaflets and public displays, manufacturers wooed female employees without previous training. The woman power campaign to enlist female employees was not restricted to the era of Rosie the Riveter.

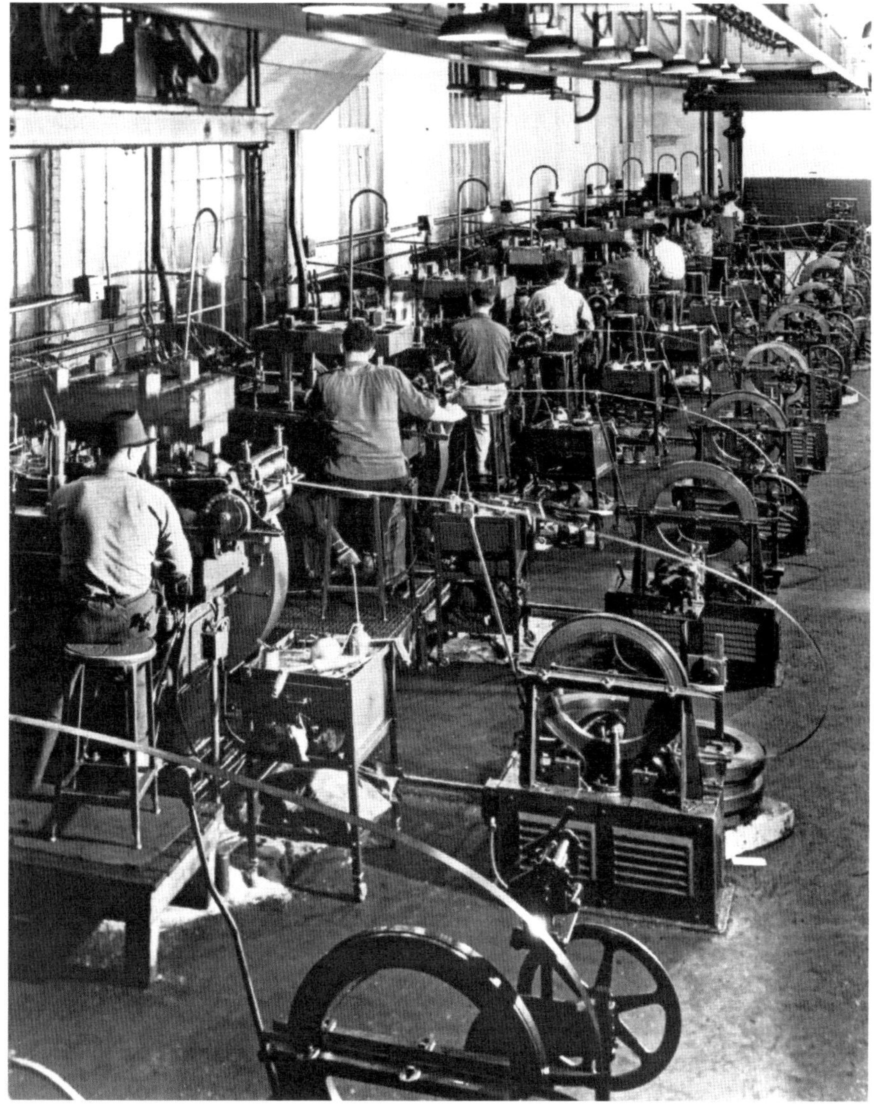

Fedders Manufacturing, 57 Tonawanda Street, bullet strip production, 1944. *Courtesy of the Buffalo History Museum, used by permission.*

Most female workers were concentrated in light industry, such as aircraft and apparel manufacturing. Curtiss Aircraft Planes, the predecessor of Curtiss-Wright, employed 1,500 women. In Buffalo, the automobile manufacturer Pierce Arrow hired 600 female workers. Another 500 women did power sewing of uniforms and assembled electrical parts.

Employers hired women for traditionally male occupations such as elevator attendants, garbage collectors and streetcar conductors. Although women war workers in overalls were doing men's work, they earned wages 30 to 45 percent lower than men's. And they didn't have the right to vote during World War I, either.

Civilian mobilization during the First World War was not limited to industry or military training camps; agriculture required temporary farmworkers for seasonal work. The Women's Land Army operated seven camps in western New York and recruited hundreds of men; women, known as "farmerettes"; and youngsters to harvest fruits and vegetables on farms in Erie and Niagara Counties.

Four days after the armistice on November 11, 1918 (now called Veterans Day), the army canceled Curtiss's contracts, and 7,000 women employees immediately lost their jobs. Over 30,000 war contracts were outstanding when the war ended. The actual number of workers displaced may have been as high as 40,000. Over 9.4 million people had been engaged in war work nationwide, and 2.25 million were women. Across the nation, nearly one quarter of the civilian workforce was employed in producing goods for wartime. For some, unemployment was the least of their difficulties because a flu epidemic was sweeping across the country, affecting twenty- to forty-year-old men and women by the thousands. Buffalo established a Civil Relief Committee and Information Bureau to provide funds for the families of servicemen. No safety net existed—no health insurance, unemployment insurance or workers' compensation for those who were injured in factory work.

Despite Buffalo's early start at war production, western New York residents benefitted least economically among all World War I war production centers. Between December 1915 and May 1918, the cost of living rose 40 percent overall. Food cost 50 percent more, clothing 75 percent, fuel and light 50 percent and housing 50 percent more between 1915 and 1918. By mid-March, over twenty thousand workers of an estimated thirty thousand western New York defense employees were unemployed due to the war's end. Only Cleveland, with sixty thousand out-of-work residents, and Detroit with twenty-three thousand suffered greater shocks.

To help the unemployed, the city immediately organized the Municipal Employee Men's Bureau. For laid-off female employees, the American Red Cross established a shop to exhibit piecework and handmade goods. A fraternal organization for Catholic men, the Knights of Columbus, offered vocational education and job placement for veterans. When the war began, the Knights supplemented the YWCA hostess house with a recreation center for servicemen on leave located in downtown Buffalo. After the war's end, the Knights of Columbus established schools to provide vocational training for unemployed veterans and non-veterans alike with twenty-three evening classes in a variety of subjects. They placed over four thousand men between 1919 and 1920. The Buffalo Knights administered the largest vocational aid and placement program in the country among chapters.

In 1920, President Woodrow Wilson signed legislation to create the Civilian Military Training Camps (CMTC) and the Reserve Officers' Training Corps (ROTC). While the ROTC program continues in colleges and universities, the CMTC project of twenty years is long forgotten. The army's youth program trained high school–aged boys in basic military skills. Fort Niagara was one of two sites (the other was Fort Drum) in New York. Over seven hundred high school boys spent one-month sessions between July 1937 and June 1940 at the Fort in Niagara County riding horses for the cavalry, practicing shooting and making beds so firm a quarter could bounce off them.

Despite the interwar tendency toward isolationism and pacifism, the army pushed for universal military training of civilians as young as fifteen years old. The Sisters of St. Francis at Stella Niagara in Lewiston ran an elementary military school for young boys with military drills and basic training by Fort Niagara personnel.

New York State was the first to legislate universal military training by ordering junior high–aged boys to drill twice a week after school. Boy Scouts were exempt. But the program was so difficult to manage that it fell apart in a matter of months. Nevertheless, the army kept a military presence at Fort Niagara.

Despite the shock of canceled defense contracts and mass unemployment, western New York remained a major military manufacturing center between 1919 and 1925, with $5.8 million in U.S. Army Air Force service contracts. Five of the top twenty-three military contractors were in Buffalo when no other city in the nation could boast of two. Although the area in the 1920s attracted industry such as rayon and cellophane fabricator DuPont to Niagara Falls, major manufacturers such as General Motors and Dunlop did not establish themselves until well into the 1930s. One reason industry was attracted to western New York was the availability of skilled labor.

Buffalo had been a pioneer in vocational education with the establishment of the first state-funded vocational high school. By 1935, seven vocational high schools provided technical education to students in Buffalo. Five of the seven had existed before 1911. But the existence of a highly trained workforce did not spare Buffalo from the Great Depression in the 1930s.

By 1930, 20 percent of western New York's population of 910,000 people was unemployed, rising to 30 percent by the mid-1930s. In 1939, the state pioneered a surplus food stamp program, arrangements for cash relief, legal provisions for group hospital plans, unemployment insurance and emergency war welfare services. Supporters called the program the "Little New Deal." Otherwise, those out of work looked to private social welfare agencies for help. Most charities closed in the first two years of the Great Depression, overwhelmed by demand.

But in 1940, western New Yorkers were relieved to be back at work after the Great Depression. For most, the war in Europe seemed far away. Besides, the president and his party were not apt to intervene. People were back to work. Life was looking up.

2

YOU'RE IN THE ARMY NOW

"JAPS DECLARE WAR ON U.S." shouted the headline of the *Courier-Express* on Monday, December 8, 1941. Buffalo police surrounded the airport with two radio cars, six policemen on foot and guards from Curtiss-Wright and American Airlines. Governor Lehman ordered all mayors to take steps necessary to prevent sabotage, and the Espionage Act of 1917 was reinstated. The navy announced that all outgoing cables and radio messages would be censored. The world changed in an instant.

My mother and father were driving out in the country on a Sunday afternoon date when the news came across the radio. Neither knew where Pearl Harbor was. My father, twenty, enlisted in the navy right after Christmas 1941 and was assigned to the USS *Juneau*, but at the last minute, he was reassigned to the Naval Air Station in Jacksonville, Florida, to airplane mechanic school. After training, he was sent to Kaneohe Air Base in Hawaii as a flight engineer testing new planes.

Keith Minthorn recalled being wounded in action at Pearl Harbor and returned to active service as a staff sergeant: "I was swimming on the beach with other soldiers when the Japs attacked. I rushed back to the air field. Several were killed running for the planes. I got my plane in the air and shot a Japanese plane. My own plane was crippled."

Minthorn used a borrowed parachute and jumped, landed on a rocky ledge—breaking his back—and was not found for thirty hours. Fourteen-year-old Joan Marie Busch Staley of the village of Kenmore recalled her reaction. "The family was devastated. We couldn't believe it that someone

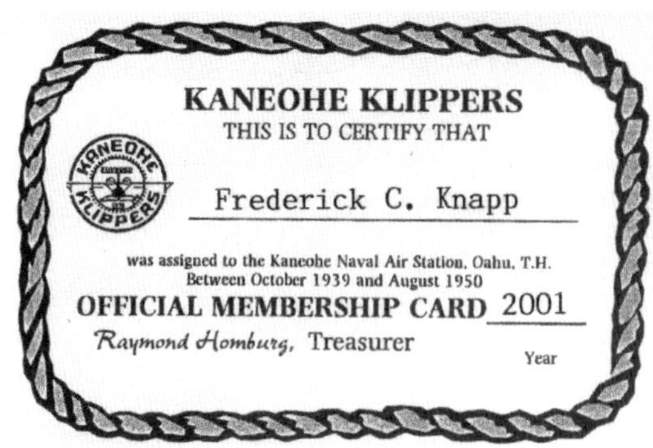
KANEOHE KLIPPERS
THIS IS TO CERTIFY THAT
Frederick C. Knapp
was assigned to the Kaneohe Naval Air Station, Oahu, T.H.
Between October 1939 and August 1950
OFFICIAL MEMBERSHIP CARD 2001
Raymond Homburg, Treasurer
Year

Kaneohe Klippers membership card. *Author's collection.*

would strike out of the blue at America. Mother was worried sick about my brother, who was drafted."

Buffalonian Albert Burghardt, nineteen, had just returned from the family home where they farmed. He heard about Pearl Harbor on the radio. "Well, I knew we were going to go in a war with Japan, that's for doggone sure." In November 1941, he was drafted into the army during peacetime and sent to Fort Niagara for induction.

Lockport native Helene Lee remembered the announcement vividly. "I was in a movie theater when they announced Pearl Harbor had been attacked. I'll never forget the sounds of men's boots leaving the theater and the soft sobbing of women and children."

Kurt Feuerherm was sixteen years old and hanging out with his friends in the Genesee-Jefferson neighborhood. A neighbor told the teens that the Japanese just bombed Pearl Harbor. "We all sort of were stunned for a minute and then we went right on playing touch football." He was drafted into the army in 1943.

Alice Smith of Middleport remembered, "I was eight years old when Pearl Harbor was hit. But I'll never forget it. It changed the world."

Leonard Amborski, a Buffalo native and Canisius College student, was visiting his girlfriend when they heard the news on the radio. "I never heard about Pearl Harbor until then, didn't know where it was." Amborski graduated in March 1943, and by May, he was teaching physics to the aviation cadets at the college. The two hundred Canisius Army Air Corps trainees graduated in August to begin learning how to fly airplanes out of the village of Clarence.

Western New York was ready for war; the entire city was mapped by police precincts. Police guarded fifty defense plants and the Central Terminal. They installed shortwave radios so that police could broadcast

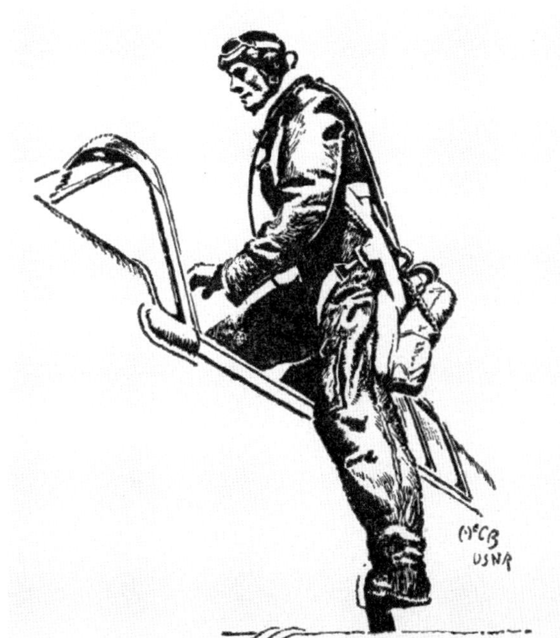

Right: Naval flyer. *McClelland Barclay, USNR, 1942.*

Below: Life in the barracks, July 1943. *Reproduction by permission of the University Archives, University at Buffalo, the State University of New York.*

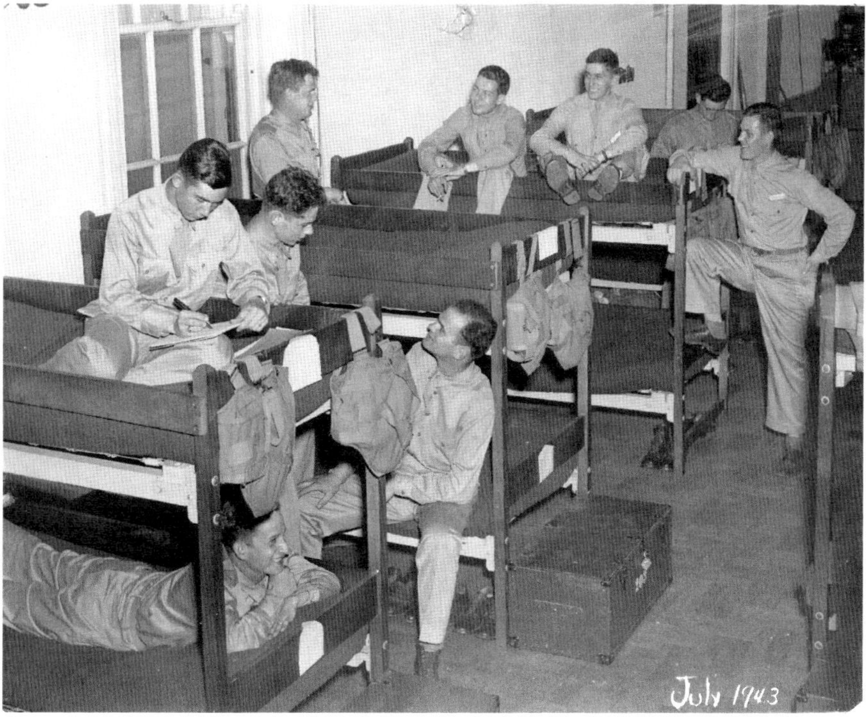

over their own station. On the day after Pearl Harbor, Mayor Thomas Holling pulled the switch of the first regular Buffalo to New York train, called the Empire State Express. He assured the populace that the city was ready for emergencies. Four hundred Fort Niagara troops guarded vital entrances at the Peace Bridge, Huntley power plant and pumping stations. At Bell, Curtiss-Wright, Buffalo Arms and Sterling Engine plants, police stopped and searched cars.

The chamber of commerce had been conducting clinics to get the small industries in Buffalo on board with defense production. Many had hesitated. But by Pearl Harbor, 50 percent of manufacturing plants in Buffalo had begun working twenty-four hours a day, six and seven days a week. The General Motors plant on River Road was converting to manufacture airplane engines and would be ready to operate within three or four months, or as soon as equipment could be installed. The Ford plant was already tooling up to manufacture heavy equipment.

Hewitt Rubber on Kensington Avenue stepped up production for self-sealing gasoline tanks for planes. Bethlehem and Republic Steel plants were at full capacity. The shutdown of the open-hearth furnaces was cut from ten to five days. Buffalo Arms, which made machine guns, went on a six-day, twenty-four-hour schedule of two shifts. American Brass manufactured ordnance parts; Buffalo Bolts, bolts and nuts; Buffalo Forge, heating equipment; Carborundum, abrasives; Chevy, airplane engines; Dupont, chemicals; Harrison Radiator, radiators; National Aniline, chemicals; Spencer Lens, optical instruments; Symington-Gould, armor plate; Trico, ordnance parts; and Worthington Pump, engines. Over one hundred other plants shaped, molded, machined and forged necessary military materiel.

Kleinhans Music Hall was the scene of a freedom rally held by the Niagara Frontier Committee for the Defense of America, bringing together racial and ethnic groups in a patriotic mass meeting. Organized labor from American Magnesium, Spring Perch and Bell Aircraft Local 501 withheld strikes.

The FBI kept watch on enemy immigrants from Germany, Italy, Hungary and Poland. These nations were either at war with the United States or under Nazi occupation. The FBI shut down Italian newspapers and radio stations in Rochester because of the possibility of communication with fascist leader Mussolini's Italy. Buffalo's foreign language newspapers, including two German, two Polish and one each of Italian and Hungarian, were spared.

The Central Terminal was packed with troops coming and going during Christmas 1941. The 174th Division arrived with 1,200 troops in

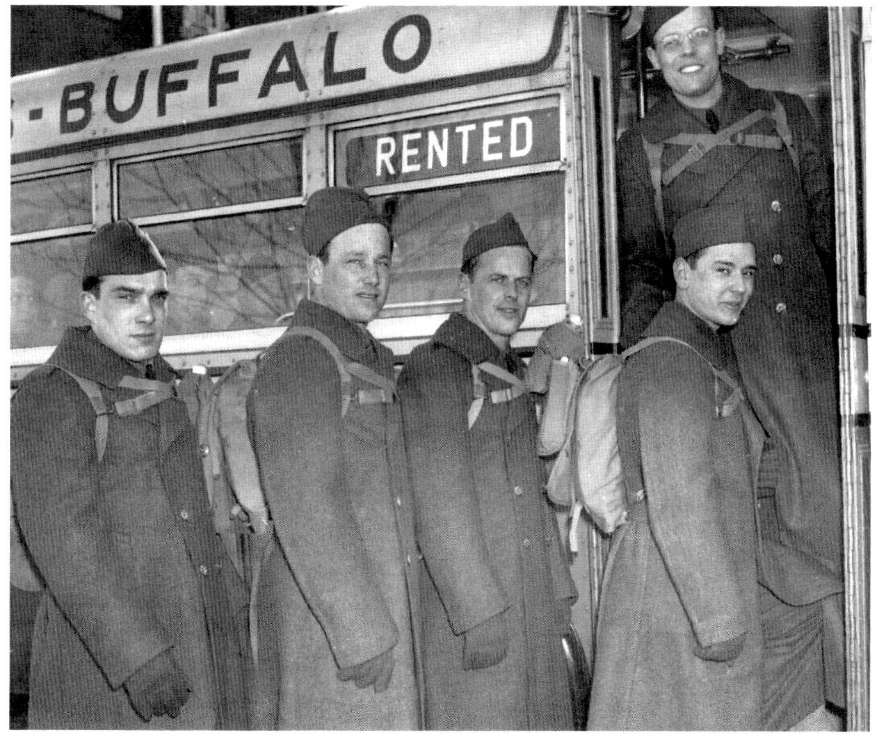

Selective Service inductees, Fort Niagara, 1941. *Courtesy of the Buffalo History Museum, used by permission.*

the morning and 4,000 more in the afternoon. Thousands of families welcomed their loved ones while others waved goodbye, wondering if they would ever see them again.

The all-volunteer 209th Coast Artillery Antiaircraft Regiment departed from New York Central Terminal to Camp Stewart, Georgia, shortly after Christmas. Some of the men were newly married. Private Jack Flanagan wed Mary O'Day five days before departure while Private Herbert Crispell, a Buffalo news reporter, kissed his wife, Viola, as they celebrated their four-month anniversary. Morale was high.

We'll lick the hell out of the Japs
And we don't mean perhaps,
We'll have them sitting in our laps
Like Charlie McCarthy.

Famed ventriloquist Edgar Bergen's dummy was named Charlie McCarthy. "This won't take us long" was the sentiment. "We've got a job to do and getting it done in a hurry means we might get back in time for next Christmas," said Sergeant Clarence B. Cummings to the *Courier-Express* reporter.

By the end of December, so many men were enlisting in the army and navy that the recruiting stations extended their hours to seven days. Their offices needed nine male typists to keep up with the paperwork. On the first open Sunday, thirty-five men were sworn in: twenty-three for the army and twelve into the navy. Oliver Work, a nineteen-year-old oil field worker, hitchhiked fifteen miles to Buffalo from Rew, Pennsylvania to join the army. Twelve men were sworn into the navy on Saturday, including Rochester brothers John and Robert Straight, who proclaimed, "Now we'll lick the Japs together!"

Whether enlisted or drafted, every man aged twenty-one to thirty-five, citizen or undocumented immigrant, had to be registered with the Selective Service on September 16, 1940. Originally, the draft was for one year of service, then ten years of reserve duty. Pearl Harbor changed all that. Every man in the armed forces would serve "for the duration."

The public approved. Historian George Flynn wrote that 89 percent of those polled said, "Older people felt it [i.e., military service] would help the boys mature and solve the unemployment problem." The men went to polling places or police stations, where the local boards of election helped carry out the process in an orderly way. Local draft boards consisted of three members designated by the governor. Advisory boards attached to each local board helped register draftees by preparing paperwork. Twelve examining physicians checked registrants for diseases. Prospective servicemen were rejected for flat feet (which later were shown to have no effect on combat duties), sexually transmitted diseases such as syphilis and gonorrhea, poor eyesight, psychiatric illness (less than 1 percent), very poor physical fitness and certain infectious diseases, particularly tuberculosis. All registrants were X-rayed, and over 1 percent showed active cases of tuberculosis. Today, Americans don't worry about tuberculosis, but the deadly disease remains highly contagious and has become drug-resistant.

The headquarters of the Selective Service was the Old Court House at Washington and Seneca Streets. Able World War I veterans from the Batavia veterans' home signed up two days after the registration went into effect. Over ninety thousand names were sent to Erie County's thirty-nine draft boards for the nationwide lottery. The first Buffalo draft was the day before Halloween on October 30, 1940. Throughout the country, sixteen million young men held their breaths as the lottery number was drawn with great fanfare from Washington, D.C. In Buffalo, the first draftee was Michael P. Gorman, who received his marching orders on November 26, 1940.

Michael Gorman passed his physical in A-1 shape. The army recruiting officer shook his hand and wished him luck. "I'm glad to go," said Gorman, "and ready to get it over with." Gorman left school after his mother died in 1928 and was working at the Michigan Limestone Company at the foot of Katherine Street when his number was called. Several of his co-draftees who had been turned down on their first exam asked for a second one. Jamestown resident Donald Okerhand, twenty-one, was rejected due to a dental exam, but after rectifying that deficiency, he returned and was included. Jacob Haver, twenty-four, could join after getting glasses for his poor vision.

Not everyone participated in the draft. Some Native American tribes did not recognize the federal government's authority and refused to register. In western New York, the Tuscarora, Seneca and St. Regis Mohawk claimed separate nation status due to treaties with the United States. Two American Indians were sought by the authorities for not enlisting, which was a crime with a penalty of a $10,000 fine and/or up to five years in prison.

Although American Indians were given American citizenship in 1924, these three tribes of the Iroquois Confederacy didn't believe this federal act applied to them. Canada took a different approach. The eighteenth-century treaties with the Iroquois Confederacy were honored, and registration for the draft was not required.

Seneca Chief Wilfred Crouse offered a compromise. Many Iroquois tribesmen registered for the draft but also asked for exemption from service. This was in line with the federal requirement that eligible men register for conscription whether they were citizens or not. But in the end, the courts did not uphold the exemption of American Indians due to separate nation status as legitimate.

Buffalo police arrested two Canadian-born Indians for failing to report for the draft. They were the first two Canadian Indians to be brought to U.S. federal trial. The judge ruled that Canadian-born Indians living in the United States were subject to induction in U.S military service. Both were of the Grand River Reservation in Brantford, Ontario. A handful of tribes had dual-nation status, but that didn't protect them from registering for the draft.

Conscientious objectors refused to participate in the peacetime draft in combatant or noncombatant status due to religious or nonreligious beliefs.

Instead, the Selective Service allowed them to volunteer for "work of national importance," such as forestry, firefighting, social service and medical experimentation. The twelve thousand conscientious objectors were sent to live in 152 Civilian Public Service camps until the end of the war. Over one hundred western New Yorkers from a variety of faiths lived in former Civilian Conservation Corps buildings. Besides a small allowance, the men were not paid by the government. The churches supported their families.

Jasper "Jay" Garner, a draftee who refused to serve on religious grounds, participated in one of the medical experiments. Garner was a member of the Church of the Brethren, a historic peace church. The thirty-six healthy young men between the ages of twenty-two and thirty-three volunteered to participate in an experiment to cut their calorie intake in half. The purpose of the project was learning the best way to feed semi-starved Nazi victims and refugees without harming them. Participants ate two meals daily as their rations were reduced over eight weeks. Garner related that he lost 25 percent of his body fat. Physicians monitored them frequently and observed physical fitness tests, which grew harder as the men became weaker. The meals resembled the types of food available to refugees: turnips, potatoes and other low-nutrition vegetables. Garner recalled the physical work of cutting wood, building fences and walking at least twenty miles daily. "We looked like walking skeletons," he said. "I will never forget those months. We all obsessed about food, food, food." Both the physical and psychological toll remained vivid in his memory.

Other conscientious objectors were sent to jail for refusing to sign up for the draft. Eight men from the Union Theological Seminary, including Joseph Bevilacqua, twenty-four, of Buffalo and graduate of Tufts University, were photographed and fingerprinted and taken to the federal house of detention in Lewisburg, Pennsylvania. The Reverend Dr. Henry Sloane Coffin, president of the seminary, said, "We have pointed out that this selective service act was framed with careful regard for conscientious objectors to military training and that to refuse to register was to refuse what any government had to ask."

Ironically, as the chaplain of Yale University, Coffin changed his mind and supported the antiwar movement during Vietnam. He accepted the draft cards of students opposed to the war and was charged with encouraging draft evasion in the 1960s but never imprisoned.

The draft initially focused on the unmarried. Single men were called first. Married men with dependents were deferred. While 1.4 million men married in 1939, over 5 million wedded their sweethearts among the eighteen- to twenty-nine-year-old group in 1940. Some of the married men were divorced when called by the draft board. At times, the wives quit working to enhance their husbands' dependency status.

Men who worked in "essential employment" were automatically exempted or deferred from serving in the armed forces. Before an army or marine volunteer could be enlisted, his draft board must sign a form to show he didn't work in a vital defense job. The navy and coast guard started checking by phone. Certain skilled workers, public officers, men over twenty-eight and farmers stayed home. My mother's cousin Balthazar "Walter" Bittner managed a farm near Arcade and was exempt from the draft. The clergy did not have to serve, but Catholic, Protestant and Jewish clergy volunteered their services as chaplains. College enrollment declined 25 percent, as students were drafted or enlisted through the Officers' Training Corps. Students in engineering, medicine, chemistry and physics were deferred temporarily until their coursework was completed. Their skills were in great demand.

No one joined the armed services for money. Fighting for Uncle Sam didn't pay well. Army privates with less than three years' service—the enlisted and drafted men—earned $50.00 per month. If they had over three years' service, the army paid $52.50 per month. Servicemen were eligible for bonuses for flight, overseas and parachute duty. Approximately 40 percent served on the homefront in noncombatant positions as quartermasters, cryptographers, camp trainers, cooks, office workers, logistics coordinators and other vital positions. At least ten men were needed to support each serviceman overseas.

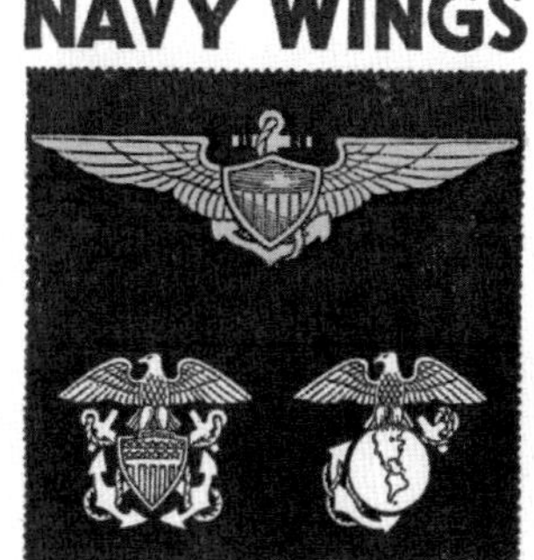

Navy Wings: What Do These Mean to You. McClelland Barclay, USNR, 1942.

The opportunity to enlist remained throughout the war. Ernest J. Kokeny, eighteen, of Depew told the recruiter, "Reason for enlisting: I want to impress the girls with a bright blue-and-red Marine uniform." He was a crane operator at Symington-Gould. "The only thing I'm worried about is that it may be a long time before I get back to Depew to show off the uniform. There must be other places where there are pretty girls!" Lockport resident and jockey Joseph Peck, twenty, refused to apply for the army cavalry.

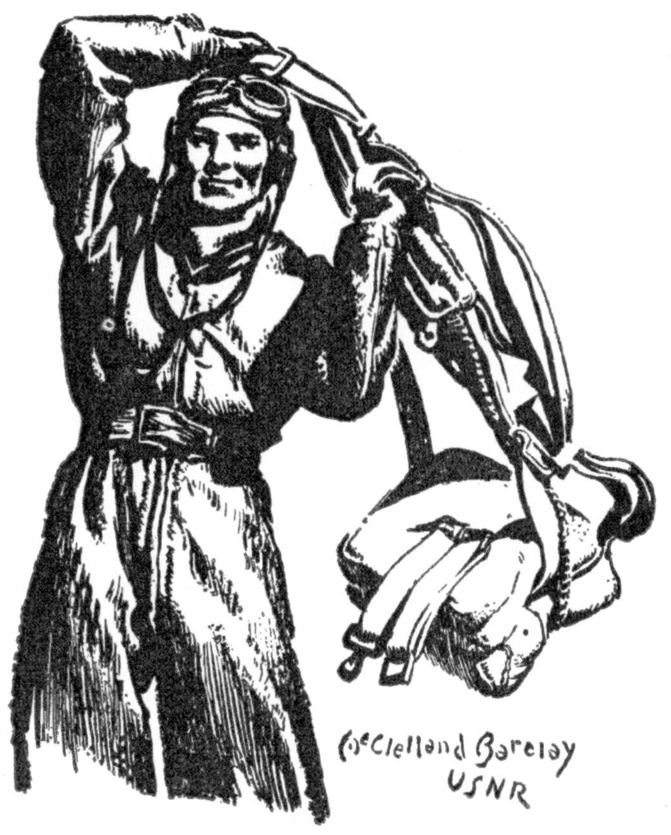

Preparing for flight. *McClelland Barclay, USNR, 1942.*

"I want a vacation from horses. Riding a winning boat for the navy should be a pleasant change."

The newspapers censored themselves from any negative comments about the armed forces from the men themselves or from observers. Despite censorship, fears of what might happen to sons or husbands drove family members to desperate acts. Myrtle Bentley, a middle-aged widow, leaped from the fourth-story window of a Delaware Avenue apartment belonging to a friend. Her two sons were in the armed services. The younger son was already in the army in Washington, D.C., and the elder was soon to be called for active duty. Apparently, that news was too much for her, and she fell to her death.

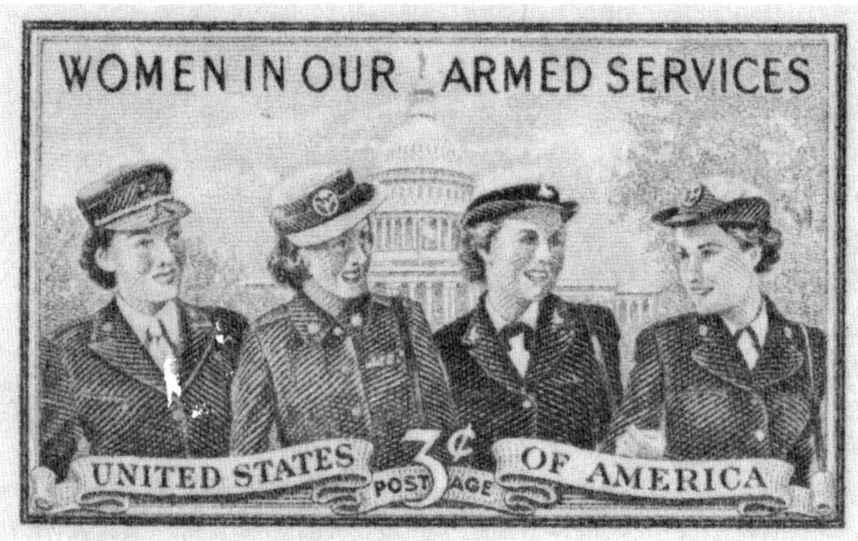

Honoring World War II armed forces branches for women. *Author's collection.*

Although parents and siblings worried about family members, they usually didn't react in an extreme manner. Men who were drafted ended up in the army infantry, and that was disconcerting enough. Enlisted men could choose from the other armed services. Parents reluctantly signed papers for boys who were seventeen years old to join the army. Since women were not eligible for the draft, they could carry out their patriotic duty by enlisting in the armed forces for noncombat positions.

Western New York women served in all the female-only armed services. Over 265,000 women nationwide volunteered to serve in the armed forces. Most joined due to patriotism, and to free men from mainland U.S. service to go abroad for combat (and not all the men were happy about that). One of the clunky ads admonished, "Be the woman behind the man behind the gun."

My aunt Rose Dold wore an army uniform as a pilot for the Civil Air Patrol (CAP), an auxiliary of the Army Air Corps. President Roosevelt founded the CAP by executive order on December 1, 1941—almost a week before Pearl Harbor. She flew in the continental United States, guarding military encampments. The male pilots had flying duty along the Eastern Seaboard looking for German submarines. Women were not allowed to fly coastal patrol missions, as that duty was considered too hazardous.

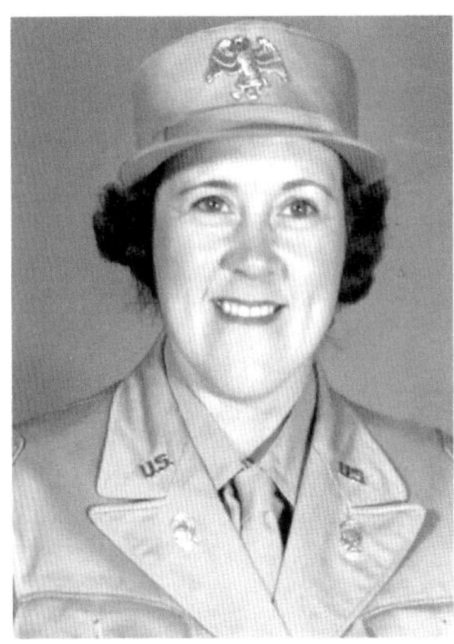

Lily Matthias Arrowsmith, WAC, July 29, 1943. *Courtesy of the Buffalo History Museum, used by permission.*

Dozens of Buffalo women like Mabell Boye and Marie Crown left to join the 150,000 Women's Army Corps who served mostly in the mainland United States. Half-page newspaper ads like "Uncle Sam needs 30,000 women for special professional technician work" described generally the type of work they did. Teachers, social workers and college students were qualified. Buffalo sent nineteen WAC recruits left to begin basic training at Fort Oglethorpe, Georgia, in mid-1943, and they were the first women other than nurses to serve within the ranks of the U.S. Army.

The WACS were sent to the Army Air Corps (40 percent) as weather observers, cryptographers, radio operators, parachute riggers and control operators. A handful were assigned flying duties as radio operators and flew on B-17 training flights as crew members. The Armed Service Forces had another 40 percent of the WAC recruits working as electricians and draftsmen. Some WACs worked in the labs for the Chemical Warfare Service, and others were trained as photographers and map analysts in the Signal Corps. This branch of the military served admirably in European and Pacific theaters.

The U.S. Navy Women's Reserves, also known as WAVES, had 100,000 women who served in office jobs in the continental United States. The "Coasties," or SPARS, was the second-smallest unit, with 10,000 women; 5 Buffalo girls and 2 from Niagara Falls were among 16 SPARS recruits leaving for Palm Beach, Florida, for training in August 1944. Most freed men from office duty.

The 1,800 Women Airforce Service Pilots, or WASPs ferried military aircraft and tested newly fixed planes. They towed flying targets to train men as antiaircraft artillery gunners, a dangerous duty. Betty June Bechtold was a WASP instructor who landed at Buffalo Airport with her brother Howard to recruit interested women.

The Marine Corps Women's Reserve was the last service established to allow women to join. The twenty-three thousand recruits mainly served at marine posts in the continental United States. At twenty-one, Theresa

Karas Yianilos was working part time at the Sugar Bowl Fountain Shop in the city of Tonawanda. Her Greek American family expected an early marriage and grandchildren. Yianilos had other plans. Defense work paid well, so she landed a position at a plant located near home, just across the Erie Canal. Yianilos hated her new job, but Buffalo's need for workers was so critical that the new Buffalo Plan stopped workers from switching jobs without a special certificate from the U.S. Employment Service. Those were hard to come by.

She was stuck, until a chance meeting with several women marines encouraged her to join them. Theresa broke the news to her parents that "the marines need women." They were unimpressed, but she was thrilled to be carrying out the recruiting poster's mandate to "free a marine to fight." Military service introduced her to the world beyond Buffalo. Male marines harassed the women no end. The least was calling their female counterparts "Big-Ass Marines" or BAMs. The women responded with "HAMs," or Half-Ass Marines. Civilians and servicemen were puzzled by the idea of women in the armed forces. Ugly rumors circulated that the women were prostitutes or lesbians. Yianilos writes in her autobiography that she was spared most of the harassment, but she may have wanted to render her account more palatable to the reader. She also wrote a column about her experiences in the *Tonawanda News*. After the war, she attended college on the G.I. Bill and ran a successful candy business with her husband and four sons in California.

In both the army and the navy, nurses also were needed at home and overseas. They were the oldest branches of the services. Shirley Devoe was an army nurse who entered the service in July 1943 after finishing her bachelor of science in nursing at the University of Buffalo. "At the hospital [where] I worked, the young physicians—they immediately finished their internships and…went on active duty," she said to the interviewer. Devoe's decision to join the army occurred suddenly when someone she loved died in action. "I just had to complete the job this young gentleman had started." Devoe ended up in Tallahassee, Florida, treating malaria, a tropical disease which she had only learned about in college, and learning how to treat airmen who survived airplane crashes.

She was demobilized in August 1946 from duty in the Philippines where she was stationed at Base "M," which had been established for the potential invasion of Japan. Devoe found she could handle any hardship that came her way. Sometimes there was one nurse or doctor for three to four hundred patients. She learned medical procedures that had not been standard in nursing school. And she made friends under adversity.

"I have friends I have not seen in thirty or forty years but we still have something in common and we still share that," she said. Army nurses received the rank of second lieutenant and received pay equal to a man of the same rank.

The Navy Nurse Corps of fourteen thousand mainly served in navy hospitals around the United States. As nurses were accepted into both the army and navy corps, their education (three years to be a registered nurse and an additional year for a bachelor of science in nursing) raised the status of nurses as professionals. As historian Yellin writes, the twenty-nine nurses in the naval hospital at Pearl Harbor ran to, not away from, their stations when the Japanese attacked. In the battle of Corregidor, seventy-two army nurses and one navy nurse were taken prisoners of war by the Japanese. The award-winning film *So Proudly We Hail* (1943) told the story of those who escaped while the nurses left behind were still prisoners of war (POWs).

3

ROSIE THE RIVETER

Upon arriving in the Central Terminal, visitors saw a massive red-and-white banner: "30,000 Women Wanted—Without Small Children." Manufacturers had run out of male labor and could not meet their production quotas without more employees. "M-Day," or mobilization day, was an all-out effort to enlist thirty thousand more female workers to join those already employed in war plants. Over half of the new employment was at Bell and Curtiss-Wright. Over 70 percent of those jobs the aviation companies determined that women could do, given the appropriate training.

A persistent World War II myth suggests that most American women were not employed before the war. But a March 1940 survey reported that 25 percent of all Buffalo and Niagara Falls women over fourteen were working outside the home in full- or part-time retail, office and light factory work. Others took in boarders, did laundry for pay, made and mended clothes, provided child care and brought in money through home-based businesses. The war encouraged those already in the workforce to transfer to higher paying defense work.

But first, the firms had to find those available for work, full-time or part-time. Volunteers canvassed door to door and block by block to survey women for their skills and experience. They knocked on doors and persuaded them to fill out questionnaires.

The western New York State office of labor sponsored a women's recruiting committee of sororities, ladies' clubs and the Young Women's

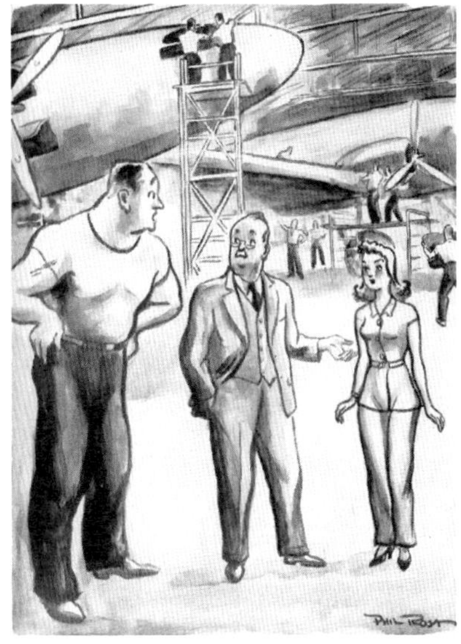

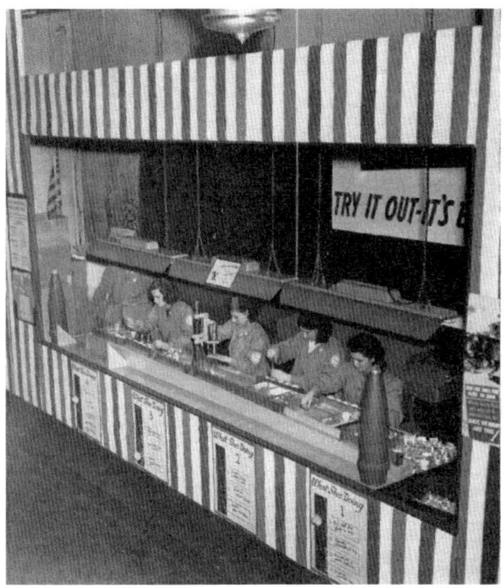

Left: *Buffalo Business*, June 1942. *Reproduction by permission of the Buffalo & Erie County Public Library, Buffalo, New York.*

Right: Domestic tasks prepared women for war work. *Hartzell, K.* The Empire State at War: World War II, *Albany, State of New York, 1945.*

Christian Association. The push to hire women came through ads in the *Courier-Express* and *Buffalo Evening News*, magazine articles, store window displays of mannequins in trousers and shirts suitable for factory work and group presentations to women's clubs in churches and schools. The state lent an open display featuring several women demonstrating how domestic skills could be transferred to factory tasks.

To attract women, plants offered inducements like transportation so they didn't have to depend on late streetcars or buses. Dunlop, which built airships, wooed women by promising a special bus traveling directly from downtown Buffalo to the Tonawanda plant with departures every twenty minutes. The all-out campaign for female workers was wildly successful. Four thousand women worked in 148 defense plants in 1941. Over twenty-one thousand women entered defense factory work within the first three months in 1942. By 1943, forty-three thousand women were working in 150 defense plants.

The Depression's lingering imprint on the area encouraged unskilled men and women to register for defense training. Over fourteen thousand persons immediately enrolled for courses in machine shop, aircraft,

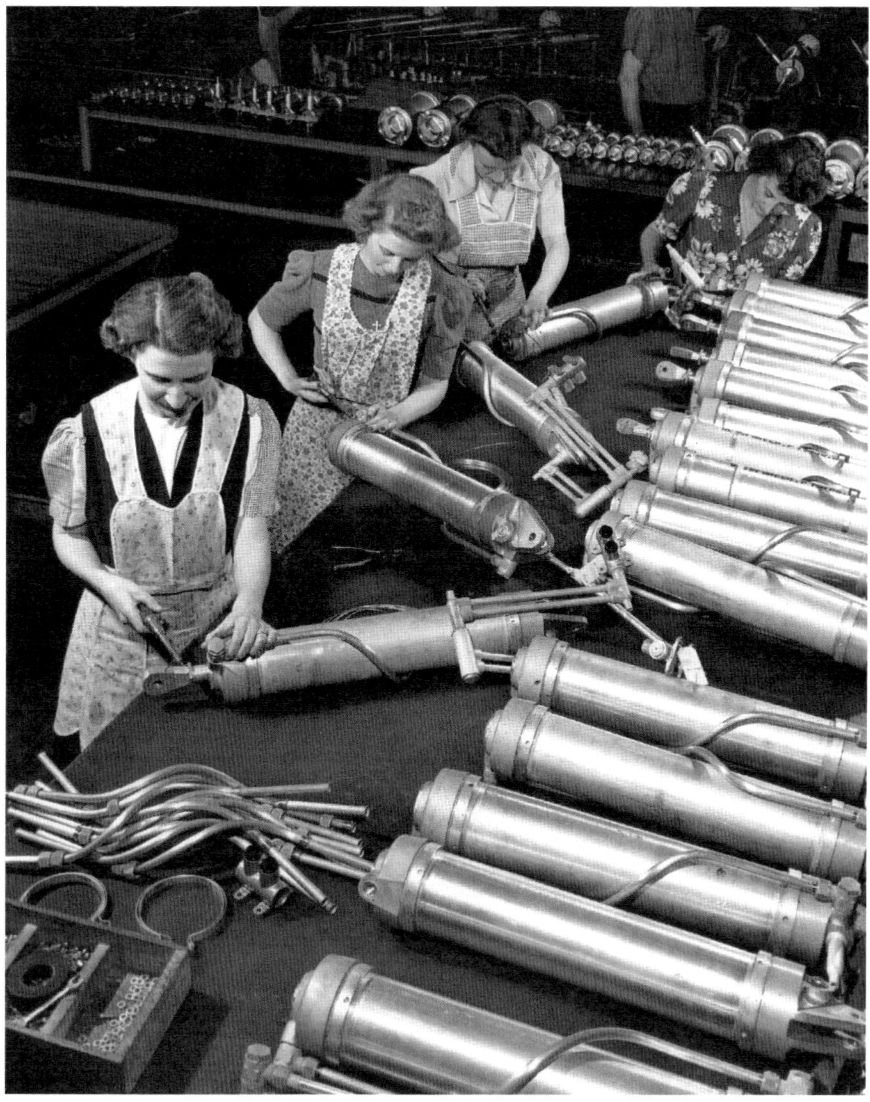

Houde Engineering, hydraulic cylinders, 1943. *Courtesy of the Buffalo History Museum, used by permission.*

drafting, blueprint reading, welding, metal processing, lens grinding and two popular classes not offered previously: aircraft mechanics and aviation.

Pre-employment sessions of at least thirty hours per week targeted the unemployed, with classes meeting from 10:30 p.m. to 6:30 a.m. five nights a week. Supplementary or upgrading training for employed defense workers was offered no more than thirty hours per week as available on five nights a week with a choice of 4:00 p.m. to 6:00 p.m. or 7:30 p.m. to 10:00 p.m. To maximize instruction time, regularly scheduled school holidays or vacation days were not observed.

The courses were popular—and free. Only half of the 14,000 enrollees could be accommodated in the newly expanded vocational programs. By November 1940, full capacity had been reached with the enrollment of 7,000 men. But shortages of applicants for the training program appeared as early as May 1941. Over 450 aircraft school trainees from outside Buffalo were placed in Curtiss-Wright and Bell, and 170 of these were from outside of New York State. After Pearl Harbor, six- and seven-day schedules were adopted by training sites to admit more registrants. Previous restrictions on the use of public school buildings, lack of sufficient funding and work hours for personnel were legally withdrawn or reduced.

Qualifications for vocational teachers and supervisors were dramatically lowered as the supply diminished. More federal money did not mean more courses. Federal funds were limited to salaries, current operating expenses and materials. The city was responsible for purchasing training equipment and constructing new buildings. The cost of instructional items specific to war production was high, if they could be found. Buffalo mayor Thomas Holling begged Curtiss-Wright to lend idle plant machinery and equipment for the aviation courses.

Vocational subjects were traditionally taught in a four-year graduated sequence, directing students into particular trade specialties after they achieved general mechanical competence. War industries couldn't wait four years. They required short, intensive courses for nonspecialists with limited technical preparation. Merely accelerating the existing course structure wasn't going to work. Shop teachers adapted regular day school technical courses into simplified, limited-skill classes. They created courses in aviation and precision measurement from scratch and wrote textbooks. Prior to the war, books and manuals on vocational topics were rare. Students learned technical subjects by observing the instructors' in-class demonstrations and practicing new skills under close supervision. Wartime state curriculum construction committees financed by federal money quickly produced a wide variety of instructional monographs for student use, then discovered that the teachers themselves needed instruction in using the textbooks in the classroom.

As war production requirements changed, so did the coursework. Buffalo's Seneca Vocational High School, the only school in the United

States with an electrically operated rolling machine, began a rolling mill operator course. The machine had been demonstrated at the New York World's Fair. Specialized defense manufacturing equipment limited what school classroom settings could offer, as certain skills required the use of in-plant settings. The Training-Within-Industry Service (TWI), another federal program, provided consultants for industries interested and able to instruct employees on the job. The apprenticeship training programs administered by the Department of Labor adapted courses for defense work. Even the remaining New Deal work relief projects of the National Youth Authority (NYA), the Civilian Conservation Corps (CCC) and the Works Progress Administration (WPA) tailored their training programs for war production work. In October 1940, the NYA established a large work center in Buffalo. Over 5,400 young persons worked at various projects based at the center during 1940, with an average stay of six months. Training focused on the skills needed by defense industries.

Although women had proven their potential for defense productivity during World War I, employers appeared to have short memories. Even the war training programs initially were reluctant to admit female applicants. Springtime rumors in 1940 hinted that women would shortly be admitted to on-the-job training. The director flatly denied them, blaming Washington for rejecting female defense industry instruction. Over one thousand men remained on the waiting list for aviation classes, but local industrialists worried that the thirty thousand new jobs projected for the next twelve months could not be filled totally by men. Governmental policy implicitly declined training women for war production jobs until the supply of male workers was depleted. Neither Bell nor Curtiss-Wright expressed interest in female workers at that time, and in fact, Curtiss-Wright had dismissed women workers and refused to consider training female employees until necessary. An influential businessman commented after touring a busy aircraft plant, "The time has already passed for scoffing at the idea of women in defense industries, or the need."

Several memory-conscious industrialists urged the training of female defense workers by evoking western New York's not-too-distant industrial past, pointing out local manufacturers had successfully employed female workers during World War I. Others pointed to the fine example of hardworking Canadian women in nearby Toronto, Ontario. The U.S. Employment Service superintendent publicly countered the ridicule experienced by women wearing factory garb and encouraged them to "pinch hit" for men as needed. Even though they ridiculed the idea, businessmen realized that several thousand women would be working in defense industries shortly. Despite the encouraging rhetoric from the chamber of commerce, state officials reluctantly concluded that Niagara Frontier manufacturers were unwilling to hire women.

The trend toward preparing women for defense work began with one of the public schools, Girls Vocational High School. In September 1940, over 1,300 young women applied for the 1,000 enrolled positions. Girls High School traditionally offered training in food service, business and power sewing. The National Youth Authority's number of female applicants started to rise dramatically as young women saw the need for work experience and, in the words of a chamber of commerce observer, saw "opportunities for their brothers and themselves." In response, the NYA began sending female students to the high school for power sewing instruction. By May 1941, the NYA had become the first program to open shop work classes in sheet metal, welding and radio assembly to women.

As 1942 ended, over 9,100 persons were enrolled in National Defense courses, including 100 African Americans and 99 women. Fewer people had enrolled for pre-employment classes than desired. The classes could hold almost 10,000 individuals, but only 1,200 were registered in July 1943. As part of the "mobilizing women campaign," interviews of unemployed applicants, referrals by personnel managers, radio and newspaper advertisements, posters, mailed bulletins titled "Are You Looking for a Job?," letters to plant managers requesting them to refer applicants for training, pleas to local unions for assistance and appeals to the University of Buffalo's placement office followed. The Erie County Department of Public Welfare "fine-tooth combed" its districts for any previously overlooked unemployed men, discovering with dismay that, where previously the jobless welcomed the chance for free training, now they preferred to be instructed *and* paid on the job. Any prospective candidates for the CCC, NYA and WPA work projects had already been referred to training programs before assignment, and the entire local NYA contingent had been placed in training. The conclusion? Train and hire the women now!

The manpower situation was unsettled further by layoffs in early 1942 as the automobile plants converted to aircraft motor production. To reserve labor for the plants' reopening, four local defense plants immediately agreed to absorb the laid-off workers and release them to their old positions after conversion. By July, the defense training schools were filled beyond capacity as women began to enroll in earnest. Aviation plants benefitted the most from female vocational training. In 1940, aircraft workers in western New York

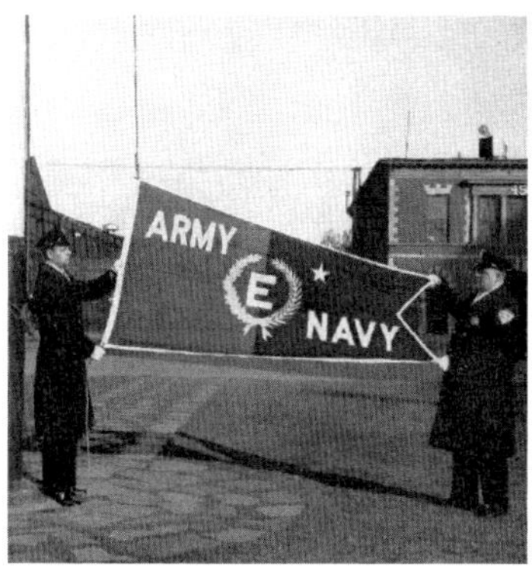

Production in high gear. *Hartzell, K.* The Empire State at War: World War II, *Albany, State of New York, 1945.*

barely numbered two thousand, virtually all male. Little did Bell and Curtiss-Wright realize that, in three years, approximately 35 percent of local aircraft employees would be female. Aviation alone would employ seventy-five thousand persons, almost 35 percent of the total war worker population.

But why did the plants wait so long to hire women? By the end of 1942, the remaining plant managers had already recruited people with disabilities, and the number of unemployed workers was tiny. In early 1943, the judge of Buffalo's "sunrise court" offered anyone convicted of minor crimes the choice of jail, banishment from the city (for the homeless) or referral to a war industry job.

Marching bands, the usual group of dignitaries and ceremonies introduced yet another campaign for defense workers in August. This all-out crusade netted 150,000 new war workers from hidden labor sources. Retirees, farmers and those in domestic service (e.g., housecleaners, maids, butlers) joined the workforce after reassurance from the state that what we would call now Social Security benefits would not be reduced accordingly. That was critical for retired men because pensions were rare.

As female employees poured into war workplaces, their previous jobs were left vacant. Since the men were in the armed services or already in defense work, employers looked to whomever was left—women who did not met the criteria for factory work—for retail and service positions traditionally filled by men. Hotels replaced—however reluctantly—male-dominated jobs such as elevator operators, servers, bartenders, porters and room clerks with women.

The Buffalo Police Department hired a female switchboard operator. Fifty women competed to fill a new policewoman position (the "Capette"), and Bell Aircraft and other plants employed female guards. The Intercity Railroad Company, which managed the streetcars and buses, hired female bus drivers and mechanics. It was a whole new world.

In 1943, State Teachers College in Buffalo (today known as Buffalo State College) trained the first female industrial arts teacher. The young woman had been working as an aircraft inspector in Lancaster. College women were

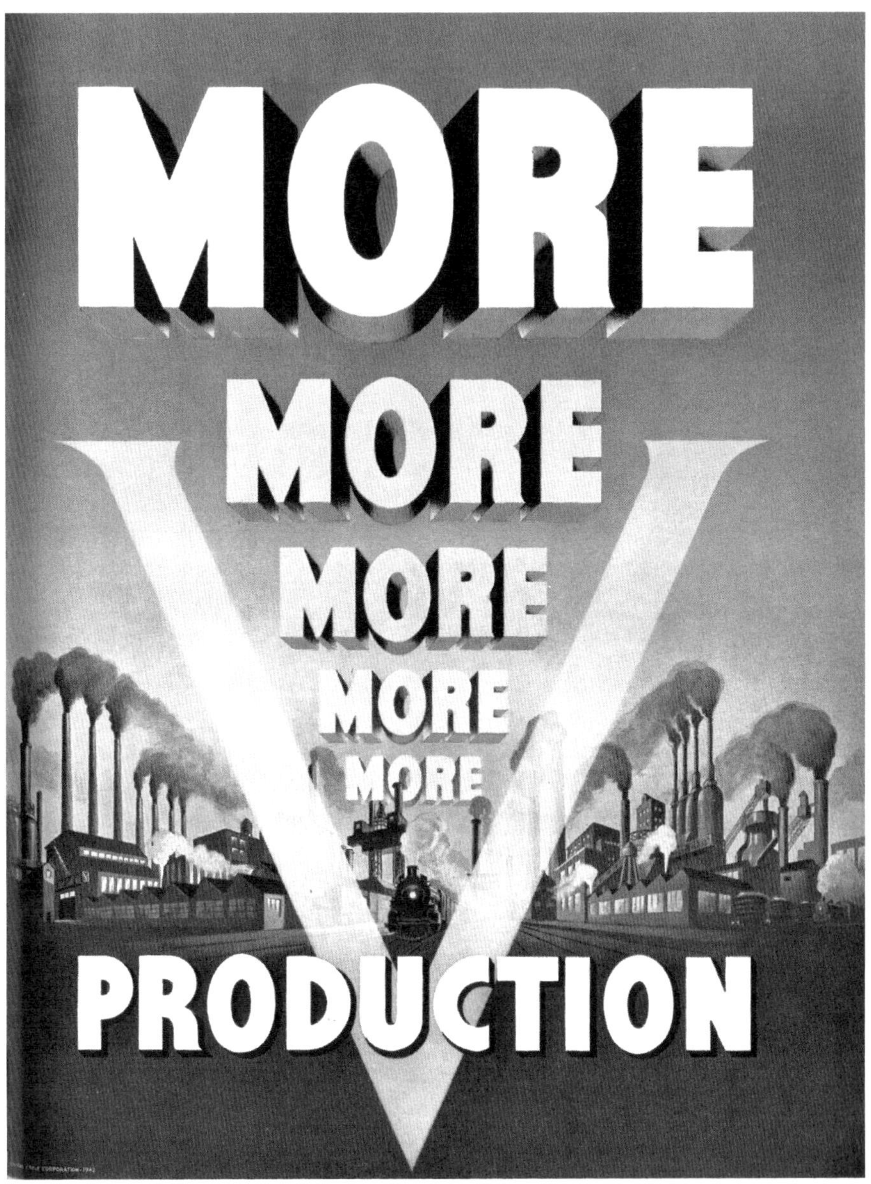

Buffalo Business, June 1943. *Reproduction by permission of the Buffalo & Erie County Public Library, Buffalo, New York.*

encouraged to enter war work during their summer vacations. After six weeks in a special training school in St. Louis, Missouri, a female University of Buffalo senior worked as an aerodynamics expert at Curtiss-Wright while her counterparts were employed as routers, truck drivers and time clerks. One of the college students was the first female employed by American Magnesium.

After female workers moved into good-paying war work, retail and wholesale stores advertised in the newspapers for sales and stock clerks. Adam Meldrum & Anderson's want ad appealed to patriotism: "Women, you are needed! Join the quartermasters of the homefront!"

Equal pay for equal work was the main obstacle, as it remains today. Not much has changed in seventy years. Michigan and Wisconsin passed wartime equal pay legislation, but New York stopped short of mandating pay equity. In a study of 550 New York plants in 1942, over 60 percent reported the same wages for men as women. One-third of the plants listed were in Buffalo and Niagara Falls. Seventeen states introduced but did not pass legislation for pay equity "for the duration" of the war.

Not until 1945 did the Federal Employment Board recommend paying men and women equally for the same work, but by that time it was much too late for the female workers who were being phased out of the defense workplace. The AFL and CIO labor contracts insisted on pay equity for aircraft plant workers. Ordnance plants in which employees assembled guns and processed ammunition—the most dangerous light industry—paid women employees less than men as if their lives were less valuable.

Employers justified lower pay for women due to family duties. Female employees were more likely to be absent from their jobs due to home and family responsibilities. Mothers without child care, and there were many, stayed home to tend to a sick child. With forty-eight-hour work weeks, women had to eke out time to do laundry, clean the house, restock the icebox so the food wouldn't spoil and shop for groceries. The grocery stores and banks were only open between 9:00 a.m. and 5:00 p.m. on weekdays. Female employees had to juggle ration cards and points to purchase food, clothes and shoes. There were long lines for scarce items. Sometimes plant managers would look the other way as workers took turns shopping for a group during the lunch break.

Even the working conditions themselves in hastily converted war plants invited absenteeism. Many plants lacked adequate restrooms for women. Few had showers, especially important for employees in greasy and dirty jobs. Unfriendly, leering or frankly hostile male co-workers and bosses lowered morale. Although the aircraft plants experimented with selling sandwiches from a food truck on the factory floor, employees had to make and bring their own meals. Day shift work made life easier to manage children and school. Afternoon shifts left young children with neighbors, family or after-school daycare. And then there were the latchkey kids, who were on their own, unsupervised at home.

Workplaces tried to combat absenteeism by appealing to patriotism in posters and newspaper ads. "Every day you don't work for the man with the whiskers [Uncle Sam], you work for the man with the mustache [Hitler]."

Not everyone was convinced that women should be working outside of the home. Newspaper articles and ads pushed the image of the married woman who placed her entire salary into war bonds as a sacrificial patriotic act. Curtiss-Wright featured an ad in the form of a letter from a Buffalo mother to her son in the army, describing how she overcame her husband's reluctance for her to work. She reassured the son that her pay would be placed entirely in war bonds. The Bishop Duffy of Buffalo sternly warned that working mothers would destroy the family. Others turned to family members to care for young children, a not always sentimental scene as described in this newspaper poem:

Grandma's Baby by Anne Campbell

Baby lives with Grandma now
That Daddy's gone to war!
The bloom returned to grandma's brow
With baby safe inside the door.
The turmoil of the war is stilled,
The troubled year has wings
There is a sweet new life to build
And hope through every prospect sings.

But most women worked at defense or other jobs because their families needed the money. According to a federal Women's Bureau survey, 20 percent of married women said they saved their paychecks to purchase a house after the war. An Italian American mother of two who worked in a war factory for thirty-five dollars a week used her paycheck to clothe and feed her two children, saving her husband's earnings against future layoffs.

The difference in pay between war jobs and unrelated jobs was striking. The New York State Division of Labor set the minimum subsistence wage for a woman at $26.45 per week, but many women earned less. Mrs. A., a clothing worker who made $26.00 a week, gave one-third of her pay to care for her mother and shared the expense of caring for one son with her husband. Mrs. DiPaolo was a poultry yard employee paid $15 a week; her husband was unemployable due to illness. Health insurance was all but unknown. There was no safety net, just limited public assistance from the city, handouts from churches and the beginning of unemployment insurance (Social Security) for a handful of industrial workers put out of work in 1941. Desperation drove people to ask for help as a last resort.

Mrs. Pauling was a married bench worker sharing support for her ill mother with two siblings. Her neighbor was a seamstress who was the sole breadwinner for elderly parents. A defense worker at Irving Airchute cared for her deaf sister. Her friend was a drugstore packer putting one son through college and another through the priesthood. Medical bills for physical and mental ailments took up a lot of income. These were the days of cash payments, no credit cards or payment plans. The waitress paying off large medical bills for psychiatric treatment she desperately needed when her son was killed in action also need a better-paying job.

Black women faced a double bar even after receiving the appropriate training. Employers who reluctantly allowed black male workers at times drew the line at black women and denied their applications. A black female applicant to Buffalo Arms complained that she had been turned away due to a heart murmur and possible tuberculosis. She visited the city clinic for treatment but was found to be in good health. Black, but not white, applicants of either sex had to submit to Wassermann tests for sexually transmitted diseases like syphilis and gonorrhea.

Here's a typical letter to Governor Lehman by a black woman with machine shop training. She couldn't find a job in Buffalo:

> *I tried to get a job at six different defense plants*
> *and each time I go to these places for work I am*
> *told they have nothing for me to do. They hire 25 white*
> *women to everyone colored. Gov. Lehman, I know*
> *I can do the work. Just as well as anyone can.*
> *It isn't fair.*

A black charwoman described the experiences of six black women employed at Bell Aircraft. "Our workbenches were separate from the white women. They had separate cafeteria seats. We had to buy us (*sic*) own tools and the white women didn't."

Irving Airchute hired black women as power sewers of parachutes through the intervention of a dentist who was an activist with the National Union League. They were segregated from the white women on the midnight shift until the Buffalo Committee on Discrimination in Employment (Buffalo Committee) persuaded the management to integrate the women and move them to the day shift.

The Buffalo Council of Social Agencies was also forced into hiring its first black employee. In May 1942, the first black women were accepted into the aviation courses to prepare employees to work at Bell and Curtiss-Wright. Even black women who already had civil service status were not hired by an ordnance plant. Under pressure from the Buffalo Committee, New York Telephone hired African Americans in Buffalo in 1943, but not as operators. By 1944, the City of Buffalo had appointed its first black policewoman. These were token "for the duration" positions.

As the war dragged on, fears of layoffs of black women led to dramatic results. Harlem's political representative, Adam Clayton Powell, visited Buffalo in May 1945. He claimed that "all Negro women here [i.e., in Buffalo] have been fired," referring to employees in Buffalo war plants. When the Buffalo Committee checked on the situation, they found that 4,400 black women were temporarily unemployed but due to return in July or August unless the war ended before that time. On a streetcar, an elderly man smacked a black woman with his umbrella when she said she hoped the war wouldn't end until she had made enough money to buy a refrigerator.

Help wanted ads in newspapers were divided by gender and race.

> *Bell Aircraft: Women wanted for specialized work on tool design. Must have some trigonometry*
> *Elevator operators: 18 to 30, white*
> *Girl* [i.e., black] *or middle-aged woman for light housework*
> *Colonial Radio has many vacancies for unskilled women in assembly inspection, light bench and machine work.*
> *Curtiss-Wright: Get in the fight, join Curtiss-Wright!*

Non-defense workers were less fortunate. These women entered the workplace out of financial need, not due to any patriotic recruiting strategies. Recruitment of labor ended in December 1943, although an acute labor shortage still existed in January 1944 and would continue through early 1945 north of Buffalo in nearby Niagara Falls and Tonawanda. The manufacturers gradually dismissed thirteen thousand workers over three

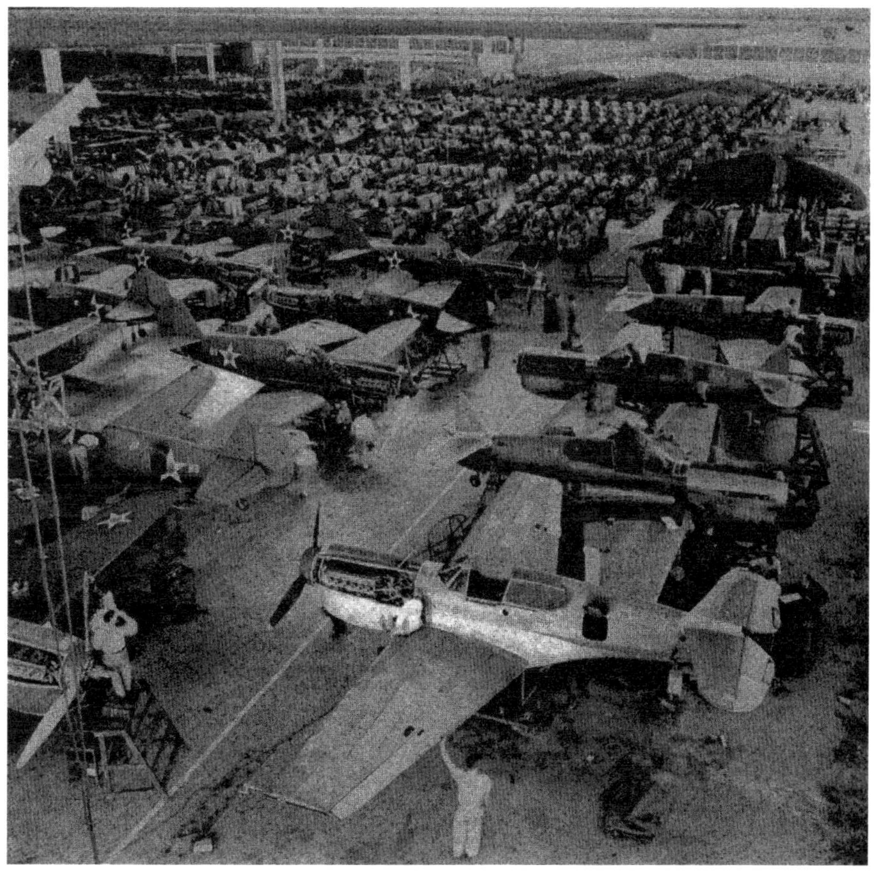

Aircraft factory. *Hartzell, K.* The Empire State at War: World War II, *Albany, State of New York.*

years, and that decrease leveled off in 1944. Absenteeism grew as homefront workers tired of long shifts and noisy plants, tedious commutes and forty-eight-hour work weeks. In June, a group of returning veterans toured local foundries to stress the continuing importance of war work, but throughout the year, western New York plants laid off large numbers of workers.

One of the earliest defense losses was Buffalo Arms, the ordnance factory that manufactured Browning machine guns and a major employer of women. Most of the two thousand released workers were directed to employment in twenty other defense plants. Last hired, female and African American employees were the first to be fired and released from large contractors like the aircraft plants, General Motors and Chevrolet. In February 1945, between three and four thousand women war workers found themselves out of work, although chemical and radio plants based in Niagara Falls and Tonawanda still needed workers. By mid-1945, Curtiss-Wright had released almost all its female production employees. Rumors that Curtiss-Wright would be moving all production to Ohio did not help matters. Bell transferred its city operations to the expanded Niagara Falls plant, but black women working at the Buffalo factory were unable to find housing nearby or transportation and were forced by circumstances to resign.

Laid-off women workers sometimes decided that collecting unemployment insurance was more profitable than accepting a lower-paying defense position. An aircraft employee earning $1.00 to $1.40 an hour was understandably reluctant to accept a job that paid $0.60 an hour. This situation became so serious that the state employment division sent investigators to western New York to collect refunds from women who refused to accept other defense jobs or contact the employment service for referrals. The local USES manager explained to the state that most of the women who declined other production work were "southern Blacks age 16 to 25 who had been spoiled by work at Bell and Curtis Wright." Such was his attitude.

Female workers were also stymied by employers who did not dispense certificates of availability in a timely fashion. Without a certificate attesting to the employee's official release from a war plant, defense workers could not be hired elsewhere. General Motors' eastern aircraft division discharged employees without certificates because they expected that the layoffs would be temporary, but the company was incorrect. Hundreds of black women workers were unable to take other positions and barred from unemployment benefits. Some released female workers blamed others for the layoffs. Blacks accused white women, and Polish women accused Italian women. At first, five black women were released for each white woman, a definite source of dissension.

After the employment discharges continued, other groups hired after native-born but before African Americans began to feel the pinch. The Buffalo branch of the National Urban League and the local YWCA helped relieve tensions, encourage retraining and persuade women to take other war production jobs despite the lower pay range.

The aircraft plants could expand so quickly during the war because the federal government had granted contracts on something called a cost-plus-fixed-fee basis. The government paid the contractors the cost of the manufacturing of the plant plus a certain percentage for profit. Having lost this status in 1945, the major defense plants tried to increase their profits by firing current workers and hiring new ones, usually returning veterans, at lower starting wages. For example, in 1943, an entry-level woman worker at Curtis Wright earned $33.80 a week, and that rose to $41.60 a week after three months of work. The profit taking by major employers in this way was substantial, and both the unions and the returning veterans benefitted from the arrangement. Both groups preferred to return to the prewar status quo.

Another reason for the layoffs may have been New York's new equal pay law, which went into effect in July 1944. Women who replaced male workers were entitled to the same compensation for the same work, but certain jobs were excluded, including farm labor.

Women also left war plants voluntarily as husbands, fiancés and sons returned from the armed forces. But over half of the available female labor was still working in 1944. This trend alarmed federal officials, who feared that women workers were seeking non-defense jobs for the postwar era, which would leave returning veterans unemployed. Many women desired to return to their homes and families, but others knew they would need to keep working to pay bills.

Defense plants reacted unevenly to the experience of women and black employees as the reconversion process began. A few, like Pratt Letchworth, planned to retain African Americans, who made up almost 40 percent of its workforce. Others, like Remington Rand and Chevy Motor and Axle, were eager to replace women workers with men, whether they were veterans or not.

According to a Bureau of Labor Statistics study that looked at women wartime workers in ten critical areas, including the Buffalo Niagara area, 114,000 women were employed in Erie County in 1944, and 67,600—almost half—had been working before the war. According to the study, over 80 percent of those surveyed wanted to continue working after the war ended. This seems to negate the popular myths that few women worked before the war, and women who worked during the war were more than eager to return to their home lives in the postwar era.

4

LIFE IN WARTIME

At noon on July 2, 1945, over 100,000 individuals witnessed the city's second invasion by combat veterans of LCT 512 (landing craft, tank) at the foot of Michigan Avenue. Here's the story told by the *Courier Express*:

> *The Navy, Coast Guard, and Marine Corps used dynamite to simulate land mines and cannon fire, and threw aerial bombs as anti-aircraft fire while 40-foot columns of water from the charges set up in the beach edge splashed on onlookers. The first wave of Marines spearheaded by an amphibious tank was brought in 1,000 yards off shore. The troops came in three LCTs which rolled onto the beach and discharged the fighters in knee-deep water. They fired machine guns and small arms at pillboxes on the beach. The LCTs returned to sea. And then the next wave came with flamethrowers putting forth tongues of flame. Sixty Marines participated while 162 police handled crowd and traffic control.*

The invasion signaled the start of the seventh war bond drive.

The United States paid for the war through taxes and savings bonds. Congress raised $147 billion by increasing personal and corporation tax rates. By 1945, over 90 percent of households sent income tax to the IRS. Before the war, only the richest 10 percent paid income tax. Excise and estate taxes soared. The excess-profits tax, established to maintain profits at levels of 10 percent of net worth, added up to a corporate tax of 65 percent. Taxes remained at this level until the Korean War ended in 1953.

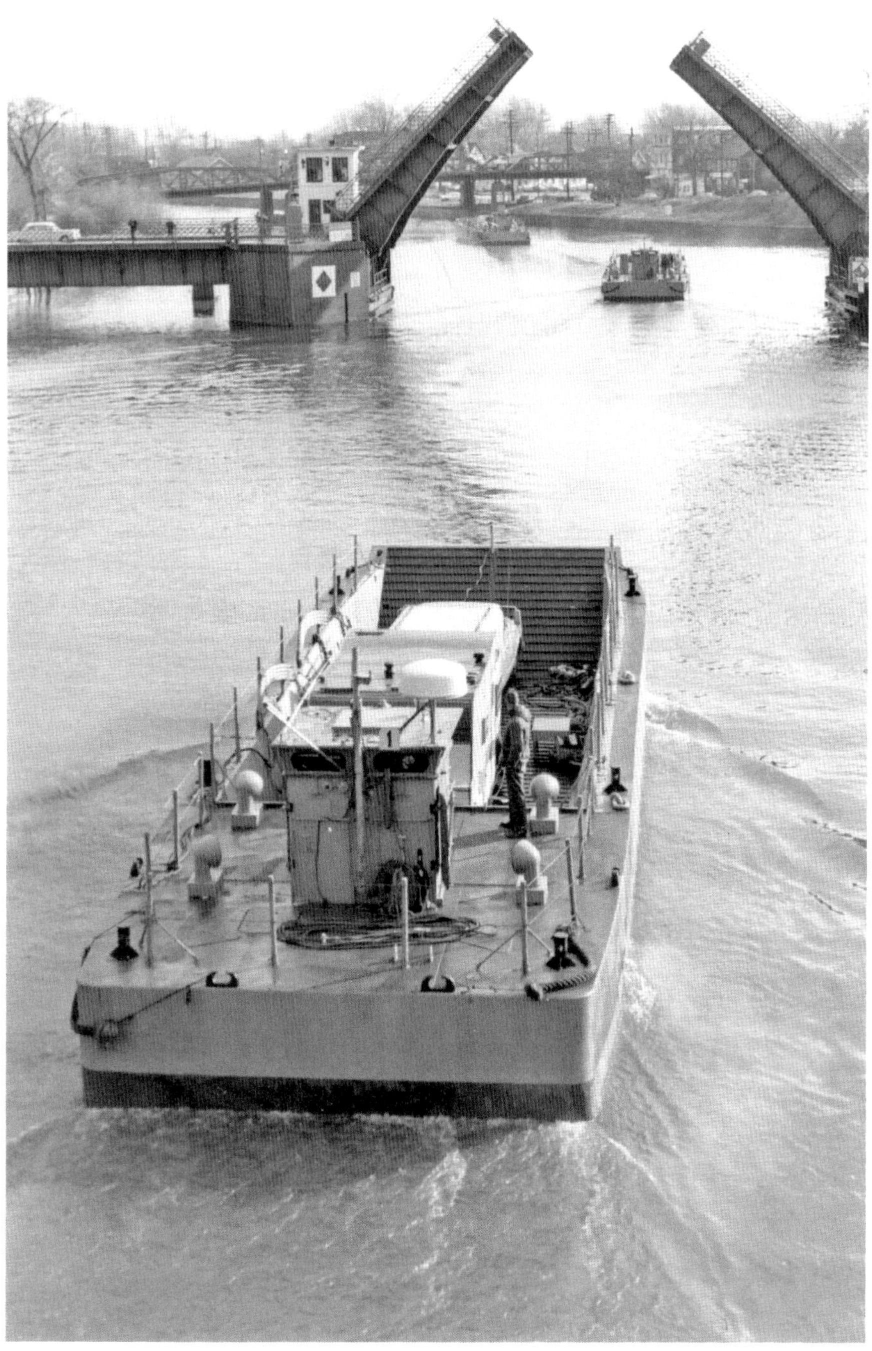

Bridge up for LCVP (landing craft, vehicle and personnel) in Tonawanda Harbor. *Courtesy of Historical Society of the Tonawandas.*

State and local governments also raised taxes to improve roads, schools and other infrastructure in outlying overcrowded communities with defense plants.

"Remember Pearl Harbor—Buy Defense Bonds" was the motto seen on posters everywhere. The Treasury Department encouraged citizens to purchase defense savings bonds to "soak up" discretionary income.

America needed money to pay for the war, and citizens responded by buying war bonds and war stamps. They gave the government a ten-year loan. The bond served two other purposes: reducing inflation, which was also controlled by price and wage ceilings, and removing money from circulation. War bonds were a form of forced savings.

Since consumer goods like leather shoes and rubber tires were rationed, or in the case of cars and refrigerators, unavailable because the factories had been converted to war production, people saved their wages by purchasing war bonds. Americans bought $186 billion of war bonds. That's 75 percent of all federal spending from 1940 to 1945. The war cost $300 billion (which in 2016 dollars is $4 trillion). War bonds were the successor to World War I liberty bonds. For $18.75, the buyer of a war bond could redeem the bond in ten years for $25.00. Newspaper boys sold $0.25 war stamps door to door to paste into war bond books, while schools appealed to children to bring their change for the war effort.

Six million volunteers sold $157 billion in bonds. Americans set aside 25 percent of their paychecks into savings, which helped fuel postwar prosperity. Thirteen million New Yorkers purchased 30 percent of the national amount. But that didn't mean that servicemen and workers didn't have money to spend on a night on the town.

The USO clubs (United Service Organizations)—not to be confused with the USO–Camp Shows, which entertained the troops in the field—provided dances, live entertainment and reading rooms. The Niagara Square Clubhouse was a favorite, with "Get Acquainted Nights" where USO hostesses danced with servicemen. The Point Abino Yacht Club in Fort Erie, Ontario, held dances for "the boys."

Crystal Beach was so busy that weekly lake rides were added from 2:00 a.m. to 5:00 a.m. The steamer SS *Canadiana* left the foot of Commercial Street six times daily. On all evening boat trips, adults enjoyed an orchestra for free dancing. A three-hour lake ride on Sunday nights came with a ten-piece orchestra, dancing and all the booze visitors could drink. Crystal Beach was the place to visit for free circus shows twice daily, including a sensational high-wire bicycle act. Ridership on the trolleys

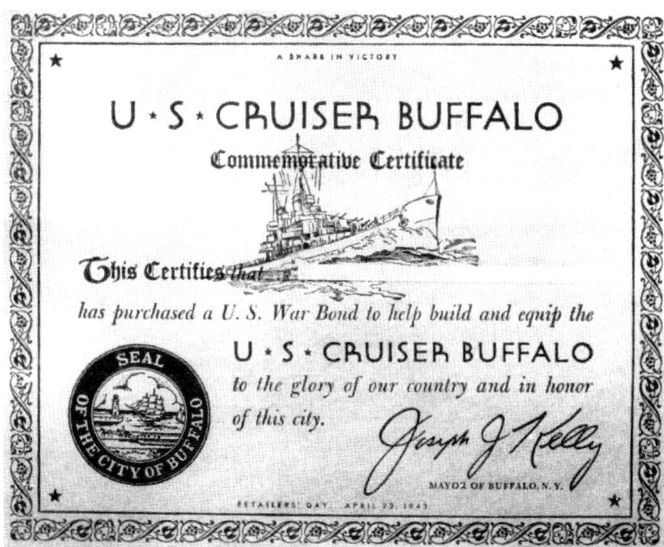

A SHARE IN VICTORY

U · S · CRUISER BUFFALO

Commemorative Certificate

This Certifies *that*

has purchased a U. S. War Bond to help build and equip the

U · S · CRUISER BUFFALO

to the glory of our country and in honor of this city.

SEAL OF THE CITY OF BUFFALO

Joseph J Kelly

MAYOR OF BUFFALO, N. Y.

RETAILERS' DAY – APRIL 23, 1943

U.S. Cruiser *Buffalo* Commemorative Certificate. *Courtesy of the Buffalo History Museum, used by permission.*

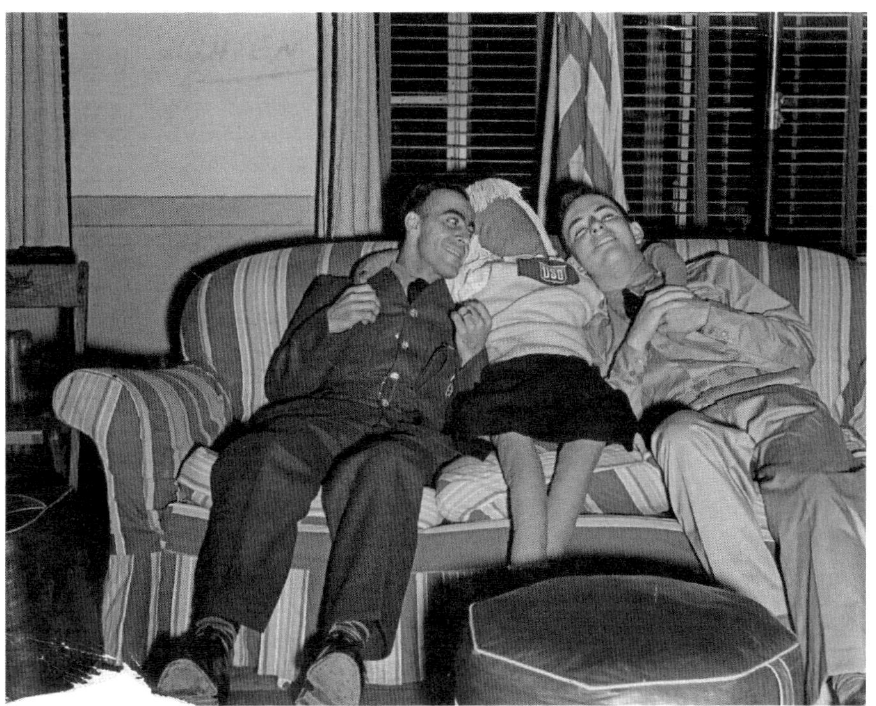

USO Club, Canadian and American soldiers with Betty Co-Ed, 1942. *Courtesy of the Buffalo History Museum, used by permission.*

and buses was surpassed only by that of Washington, D.C., bragged the *Courier Express.*

Buffalo's movie theaters entertained soldiers on leave and off-shift defense workers. *Follow the Boys,* a musical romance with an all-star cast, played at the Lafayette, followed by *Twilight on the Prairie,* a musical western. Theatergoers left humming "Let's Love Again," "I Get Mellow in the Yellow of the Moon" and "Where the Prairie Meets the Sky."

Shea's theater advertised *Sensations of 1945* with stars Eleanor Powell, W.C. Fields, Sophie Tucker, Woody Herman and Cab Calloway. Many theaters highlighted having air conditioning, which was a draw for war workers stuck in hot factories all shift, especially in the summer. Dipson's Franklin on Ridge Road in Lackawanna showed *Angels over Broadway* with heartthrobs Douglas Fairbanks Jr. and Rita Hayworth. Fred MacMurray starred in *Rangers of Fortune* at the Riviera in the Tonawandas.

And then there were sensational movies. At the 20th Century, the feature film was *Are Those Our Parents?*

> *Scandal in the home! It's the scorching lowdown! Why blame teenagers for the crime and pleasure jag that's packing our jails? See the real guilt of excitement-craving grownups!*

But today's readers are more familiar with *Going My Way* with Bing Crosby at Shea's Great Lakes and *Double Indemnity,* a Billy Wilder suspense film with Fred MacMurray at the Hippodrome.

Besides a long list of movie theaters, dinner clubs and radio shows were popular. The Stork Club in Buffalo on Seneca Street featured Dorothy Dale, "Tap dancer extraordinary." Newly constructed Glen Park Casino had a parking lot for one thousand cars. Patrons enjoyed the restaurant and a show. Restaurant Chez Ami on Delaware was the place to take a special date for fine dining and dancing. The Mad Hatters Club at Niagara Falls Boulevard and Ward Road gave visitors a comedy revue.

But two favorite clubs stand out. The Palace Burlesk at Main and Niagara in Shelton Square featured lovely Nancy Blair, the "Gee, I like you" stripper; "A Hit in Legit" Ann Corio and her thirty-six Girls in Blue; and the elegant Gypsy Rose Lee. Several clubs offered female impersonators. Dewey Michael ran the club for more than fifty years, until its closure in 1967. Ten years later the club became the Studio Arena Theatre and later the 710 Main Street Theatre.

The other venue was McVan's on Main and Hertel, which held "V for Victory" revues: Maya Keila, Oriental dancer; Alice Noonan, tap dancer and baton twirler; the eight dancing McVanettes; and Jimmy Foster, a NBC radio star. From Frank Sinatra to rock bands in the 1970s and '80s, McVan's was the place to enjoy new talent.

During the war, the night clubs reported a 50 percent increase in business, but according to a club owner, "Good waiters are scarce and so are china and glassware. Good bands are broken up by the draft." Despite his complaints, the best of live entertainment visited the city. Woody Herman and his band, "The Band that Plays the Blues," amused large crowds seeking the big band sound.

For those seeking more exciting entertainment, the New Memorial Auditorium offered "Hell on Wheels," a roller derby contest (reservations needed). Professional hockey, the Bisons' debut in the American Hockey League, began in late 1940. The World's Greatest Wrestlers, "Don George vs. Rasputin," or for the second card, "Iron Talun vs. Sandy O'Donnel" entertained four thousand customers at the New Memorial Auditorium for fifty-cent tickets

In between shifts, employees enjoyed radio shows from WBEN, WEBR, WKBW, WGR and WBNY—call numbers familiar even today—from 7:00 a.m. to 11:00 p.m. on Eastern War Time. WBEN's morning show began with Clint Buehlman, who would become a fixture of the popular show into the 1970s. Adults liked listening to the Fred Waring orchestra, news by Lowell Thomas and the crooning of Bing Crosby. Children eagerly turned on Dick Tracy, Tom Mix the cowboy and Superman. Soap operas included *Guiding Light*, which smoothly made a transition to television and became the longest running show of the genre. *Queen for a Day*, Kate Smith the singer, and Betty Crocker amused the ladies.

Actress Bette Davis captured a woman's reflection on the dating scene by singing, "They're Either Too Young or Too Old." For every popular song such as "Praise the Lord and Pass the Ammunition," "As Time Goes By" and "It's Been a Long Long Time," there were those that didn't last the test of time: "Ma! I Miss Your Apple Pie," "A Boy in Khaki—A Girl in Lace," "There's a Blue Star Shining Bright" and "Angels of Mercy." The "blue star" refers to the small banners in the windows proclaiming that a member of the armed forces lived there and was on duty. (Should the worst happen, a gold star appeared instead.)

Even the servicemen overseas appreciated Buffalo's generosity. Three Kenmore men and one Buffalo boy were serving in New Guinea. They wrote sportswriter Billy Kelly for a few smokes (cigarettes). He sent fifty cartons from the Buffalo Jaycees. "We Kenmore and Buffalo boys do a lot of bragging in our outfit about the God's country we came from," the servicemen wrote back, "and the people of Buffalo back up that bragging!"

Advertisements like this summarized the spirit of the homefront activities:

Are you in the war 100%?
Does your war effort add up to 100%?
Do volunteer work?
Buy war bonds?
Give blood?
Save tin, fat, paper, fuel, and tires?
Observe ceiling prices, pay ration points?
Buy nothing you do not need?
Write often and cheerfully to servicemen?
Have a victory garden?
Repeat no rumors—guard your talk?

While upper-class men retired to the Saturn Club, "Where the women cease from troubling and the wicked are at rest," working men and women wanted more than a place to relax. Those working second and third shifts needed extended hours for services like grocery shopping, banking, barbers and beauty shops, medical service and other essential functions. In Buffalo, a council composed of local unions and management convinced businessmen to retain a percentage of their bargains until the evening for female defense workers, but only sporadic attempts were made to provide other services.

Just before Pearl Harbor, the American Women's Voluntary Service established itself in Buffalo, much to the annoyance of the Buffalo War Council, which found the program duplicating the work of existing agencies, like the Knights of Columbus. The Buffalo chapter set up a canteen. When the Buffalo Council protested again, the Erie County War Council invited the chapter to continue its work, claiming that the county was supreme over the city. The truth was that prospective members had little time for outside activities. The answer was usually no for young mothers with children. One young mother may have to prepare meals for her children at the usual hours, another for her husband after the second shift and have another meal for her brother besides trying to keep the children quiet while the men slept. But women volunteers were needed to staff information booths, knit bandages for the Red Cross and take first-aid courses.

The Erie County and Buffalo War Committees eagerly sought volunteers for civilian protection. Applicants filled out a detailed form asking for information that today we would find either unnecessary or illegal: religion, parents' birthplaces and a comprehensive range of abilities sought and training desired. Volunteers were needed as switchboard operators, script writers, civil engineers, male nurses, steam fitters, bicyclists, folk square dance instructors and—yes, those with the skill of "communication by pigeon."

Air raid warden was by far the most important job. Homes and businesses had black air raid curtains that kept light from penetrating to the outside. Those outside during a blackout were to dim any sources of light. Williamsville resident Carol Schmeidler's grandmother Celia Slohm (Bernstein) was an air raid warden in Buffalo. Her identification card from the U.S. Army's First Interceptor Command featured her photo and fingerprints. Scheduled and advertised blackout drills forced people to practice their response to the air raid alarm signal—a series of intermittent siren blasts, initially from fire trucks. Air raid wardens supervised the blackout drills, walking or bicycling up and down neighborhood streets to make sure no light that might attract enemy bombs escaped around the windows and that inhabitants had pulled down their blinds. Drivers pulled over to find cover in the nearest building. Street lights were put out. Although the wardens could fine anyone who violated blackout rules, they issued warnings.

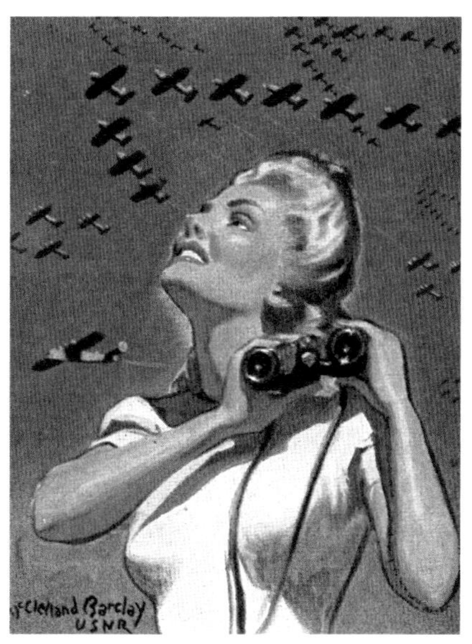

Civilian defense volunteers learned how to spot enemy airplanes. *McClelland Barclay, USNR, 1942.*

In the village of Kenmore, the process of extinguishing and relighting gas street lights was expensive and took all day. The village board of trustees was relieved to find blackout covers for the street lights that could be lowered and raised by a handle that anyone could operate. The cost of the village blackout was one dollar per light, but the village lamplighter and his assistant were unhappy at the extra workload.

Over 30,000 volunteers signed up for duty in the city of Buffalo, including 21,742 air raid wardens.

There were 150 public air raid shelters to hold 100,000 people and 2,450 auxiliary fire corps with special equipment (e.g., pumps, helmets, ladders and gas masks). Decontamination gas protection squads had gas masks and protective clothing. All fire department staff, school department officials and theater ushers received gas and bomb training, while others signed up for demolition and clean-up crews. One hundred emergency medical service teams were ready in 35 casualty stations, and the control center warning center was ready for use.

Brigadier General Willis R. Taylor, the commanding officer of the First Fighter Command, appealed to women to volunteer with the Buffalo Warning Center. "They chart information on every plane that flies through the area," he said. "I cannot overemphasize the importance of the Buffalo area. Your concentration of war industries and Great Lakes shipping combined with your proximity to Canada dictate our present action."

The village of Kenmore took Taylor's advice seriously, erecting a spotting station at the corner of Delaware and Legion. Spotters used binoculars to match the shapes of planes printed on playing cards to what they saw in the air. The plane outlines were viewed from the side or the bottom.

Author Richard J. Lingeman painted Buffalo's civilian defense program as woefully, if not ridiculously, unprepared. According to a 1942 *Harper's Magazine* article, Mayor Joseph J. Kelly allegedly bungled the practice blackout scheduled for December 1941. The city police, air raid wardens and vital equipment, such as flashlights, were unavailable. Fire engine sirens fizzled. End of story. This report, repeated by other historians, always puzzled me. The first air raid in Buffalo was in December 1940 under Mayor Holling and presumably went well. The Buffalo City Council blasted the journalist, describing the event as "perfectly carried out," but President Roosevelt sent his sympathy to Mayor Kelly. In any case, the *Harper's* story did not raise Buffalo's reputation as being well prepared for the war.

The mayor had his own problems. Kelly, a Democrat, was at war with the Republican Common Council over city jobs remaining unfilled. The collection of garbage and ash (from coal furnaces) was down 25 percent. The sanitation department had already changed the monthly trash pickup days from seven to nine. The council agreed to reclassify 3,500 employees to raise their salaries so they wouldn't be tempted to leave for higher-paying defense jobs. Kelly's popularity dropped further when he ordered a five-and-a-half-day work week at city hall, including Saturday mornings.

In 1943, the mayor's committee on recreation began to consider the subject in a systematic way. The committee tried to coordinate the activity of three USO centers, which provided free theater tickets, home hospitality and free use of all YMCA facilities to all uniformed services servicemen. Providing recreation for shift workers was more challenging. The YMCA nearest to large war factories along the Niagara River was open twenty-four hours a day.

The USO was formed in 1941 by six religious social welfare agencies: the YMCA, the YWCA, Jewish Welfare Board, Salvation Army, Travelers Aid and the National Catholic Community Services. The USO was totally administered and financed in conjunction with the federal government. That is, the USO broke the separation of church and state for wartime. The USO's priorities were servicemen and women and their families. In 1942, services to defense workers were included. Today, the USO is often confused with its entertainment-oriented counterpart, USO–Camp Shows, which provided music, theater and sports demonstrations to servicemen and army camps, naval stations and hospitals. Bob Hope and other professional entertainers served with USO–Camp Shows, which was affiliated with the USO only for the purposes of finance and administration. Discrimination due to creed or race was forbidden but not by gender. Many USO clubs did not welcome servicewomen because local women's clubs were perceived as the proper sphere of recreation. Concern over fraternization between servicemen and servicewomen probably underlay the reluctance to admit WAVES, WACs, WASP, women marines and SPARS, although officially the USO did not prohibit them. Some USO clubs set aside a portion of the facility for the exclusive use of servicewomen. Black servicewomen were doubly barred. USO centers were segregated because of local regulation or by the request of African Americans who didn't want the tensions that arose when they entered the USO clubs. By 1943, 188 of the 1,326 USO operations were designated for blacks.

Buffalo's USO-type club began as a Knights of Columbus service club in 1940, the first of its kind in the nation, a rest and recreation center located in the heart of downtown Buffalo. The club was conveniently situated across the street from the train station where men left for induction at Fort Niagara. In 1942, the club was eclipsed by a USO club stationed several blocks away. By September 1942, over thirteen thousand people, including servicemen, servicewomen and war workers, enjoyed the USO service monthly. Two other USOs operated in Buffalo. Both were troops-in-transit lounges situated near the train stations. Beginning in 1942, the Salvation Army sponsored a small USO next to Fort Niagara for servicemen and their visitors. Those who disliked the USO described personnel as "belligerent,

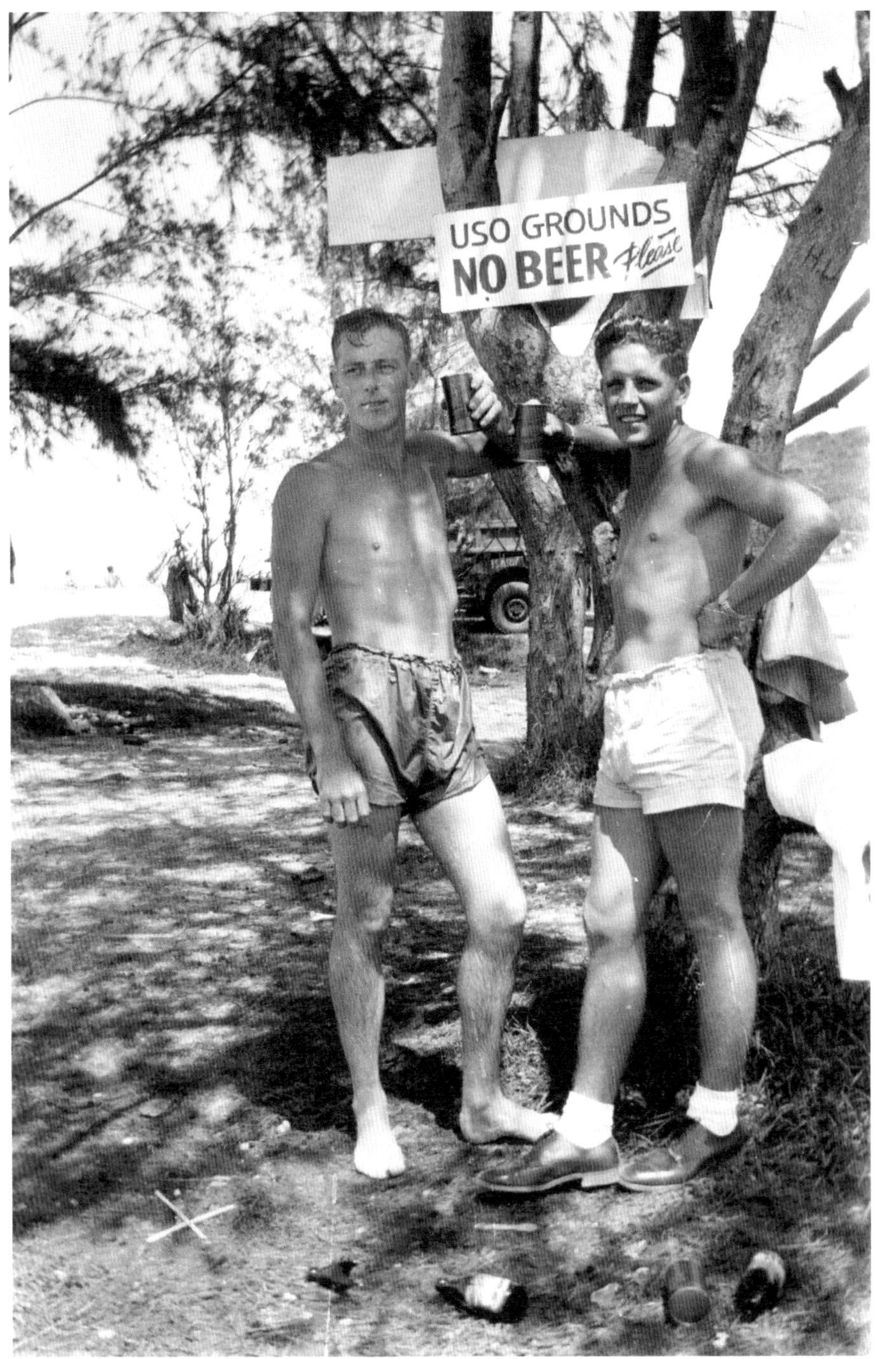

Territory of Hawaii, 1943. *Author's collection.*

insensitive to local conditions, uncooperative, undertrained, inefficient, and over-salaried." Old-time residents resented the special services offered to newcomers and claimed that the USO's program divided the community between permanent inhabitants and transient newcomers.

Much of the criticism was directed at programs for war workers. Overcrowding severely strained recreational facilities as tired but well-paid defense workers flocked to movie theaters, parks, dance halls and saloons. "We prayed for this thing and now we are praying for forgiveness," lamented one mayor, bemoaning the impact of total war on his community. Serving defense war workers was an unglamorous job that did not easily attract volunteers. The industrial USO required the cooperation of the major defense plants, which was not often forthcoming. Some industries were unhappy that the national religious social welfare organizations provided recreation instead of the federal government. In Niagara Falls, bitter disputes between the USO run by the Salvation Army and the American Women's Voluntary Service resulted in the latter running the canteen, although the center had no official ties with the USO.

But out in the fields of war, the USO might provide an oasis, however small, of a cold drink and a chair or the chance to meet new friends.

Buffalo's two main newspapers—the *Courier-Express* (mornings) and the *Buffalo Evening News*—still ran social and women's pages as if the war was not happening. Ads for clothes focused on styles that used minimal fabric, shoes were heeled with hemp or cork and recycling or repurposing prewar items was encouraged. Menus were tied to rationed foods and tight budgets. Here's a recipe suggested by the (probably desperate) food editor:

> *Sausages baked in bananas*
> *6 unpeeled bananas*
> *6 to 12 small link sausages (12 to 16 per lb.)*
>
> *Slit bananas lengthwise to form a pocket and place 2 sausages in the slit. Arrange with the slit side up and bake at 375 degrees in a moderate oven 15 to 20 minutes. 6 servings.*

The newspapers printed the latest rationing instructions. In 1942, the federal government set price limits on many items and rationed food to keep consumers from hoarding and to make sure everyone had sufficient supplies. To buy rationed items, residents needed war ration books (food coupons) filled with stamps to buy "blue point" foods that were processed

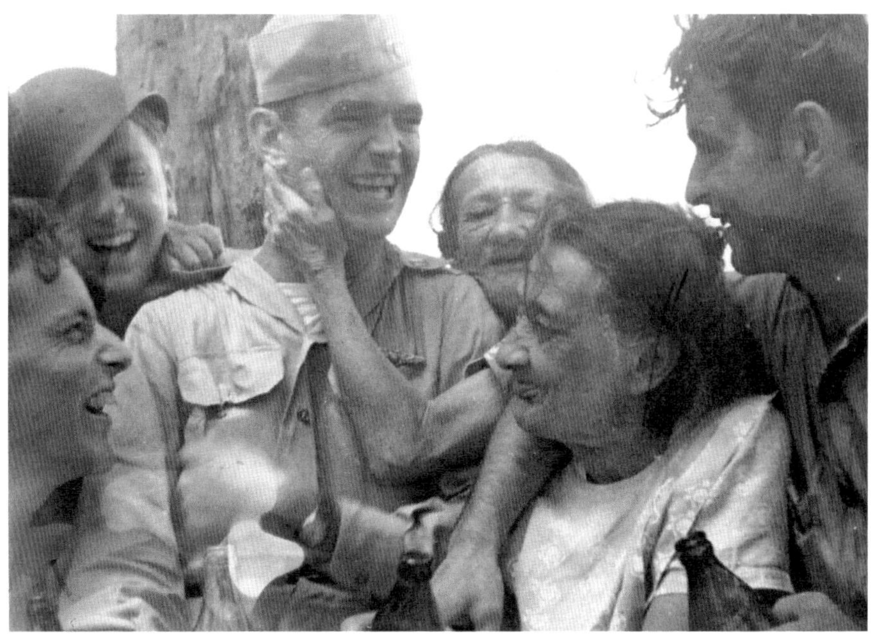

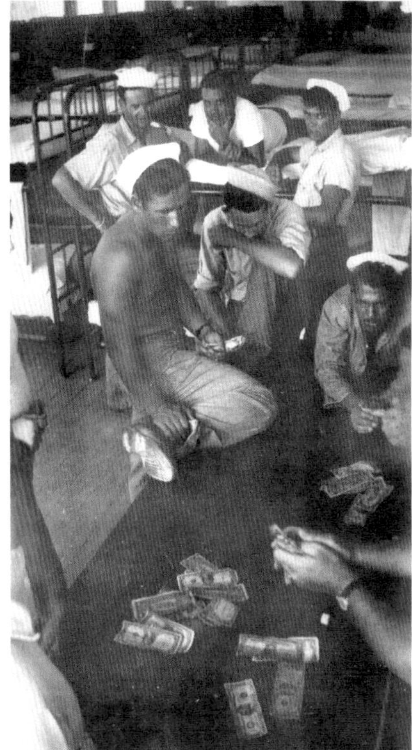

Above: Don't mind the USO, Kanehoe Airbase, 1943. *Author's collection.*

Left: Sailors playing craps. *Author's collection.*

and "red point" fresh foods like meat, fish and dairy. The stamps were good for a month but didn't guarantee supply. Consumers saved points for hard-to-get rationed items like sugar and coffee. Periodically, the government changed the value of points as supply and demand made necessary. For those preparing food at home or in restaurants, rationing was a complicated and frustrating problem.

A black market quickly sprang up to trade ration stamps or forge them. Some enterprising thieves would steal high-demand items like meat and resell them for high prices. The attorney general ordered a crackdown on black market operations in Buffalo. The food racketeers raked in thousands of dollars daily. Six meat markets possessed ungraded (i.e., illegal) beef, veal and lamb. Inspectors used a "follow-the-cow" tactic to track down violators and fine them. Even though consumers knew that food shortages were linked to the black market, they still bought the coveted foods.

Shoes were the most sought-after clothing item subject to rationing. Leather was provided to the armed forces but not the consumer, and wartime shoes made of stiffened cloth and glue fell apart easily. The Kresge stores in Buffalo were suspended for several weeks for selling shoes in violation of the rationing rules. Silk cloth and stockings were off the market, to be used for parachutes, so until nylon stockings were available, women painted their legs or used eyebrow liner to draw a seam up the back of their legs.

Motorists complained about gas and rubber (tire) rationing, but the Japanese Imperial Army controlled routes to Indonesia from 1942 to 1945, creating a shortage of rubber that affected American production. Here's a light-hearted look at the frustrations of not being able to use a car from Edmund Kiefer's "Spur of the Moment Column" in the *Buffalo Courier Express* (1942):

After the war is over
After the rationing's done,
Any car will be a wonder,
No end of novel fun.
Radical changes are welcome
But who'd ask for anything more
Than to stay at the wheel
And not feel like a heel
After the war!

5

BRINGING IN THE SHEAVES

Life during wartime also meant defense work having nothing to do with a factory. The secretary of agriculture declared that agriculture was the most important industry, and indeed, foodstuffs were vital to the Allies. Lend-lease contracts extended beyond aircraft and other defense equipment to certain agricultural items desired by the Allies, including dairy products, eggs, lard and hogs. In 1941, the first signs of farm manpower deficit appeared, a reduction in agricultural labor that reached 20 percent between 1940 and 1941 partly due to the draft. The federal agencies cooperated with youth groups as a source of seasonal labor. By the end of 1941, Selective Service had designated draftees from certain areas of the county as deferred because agriculture was considered an essential industry to the war.

Experienced farmworkers left the farm for high-paying city centers. After 1942, the department of agriculture took over the recruitment and placement of farmworkers, delegating this activity to the county level through the extension service. Throughout western New York, the full range of labor sources was represented. Housewives, white-collar workers, high school and college students, teachers, migrant workers, servicemen on leave, foreign nationals from the West Indies and German prisoners of war were involved in agriculture. Nearby residents whose occupations left summers free, such as teachers and students, were recruited first. New Yorkers across the state were willing to give up at least two weeks of vacation during the late summer and early fall to travel to the Hudson Valley, Finger Lakes and western New York to pick vegetables and fruits and process food in canneries. They were housed in tourist cabins and farm labor camps or on individual farms, and the government paid for transportation.

Freshman and sophomore female students from state teachers' colleges at Brockport, Buffalo, Cortland, Fredonia, Geneseo, Plattsburgh, Oswego and New Paltz were released from late spring and early fall classes to help with harvesting in critical areas, such as Niagara County. Several colleges, such as the Fredonia campus, closed briefly during September and October to enable students and faculty to help farmers and canneries to process the grape crop into juice, jam and jelly.

New York State's farm cadet victory service registered and placed students fourteen years of age and older on farms during summer vacation. Vacation work on farms during wartime was a patriotic job, reminded the Future Farmers of America. Three types of farm service were available to cadets: day hauls, work camps and live-ins. Day hauls or working for a day only were the most common type of farm employment, and 75 percent of all cadets worked daily. Farmers picked up groups of students in the early morning from collection sites and returned them in the evening. Only 10 percent of farm cadets lived in farm labor camps.

Over sixty farm labor work camps were established by farmers to house students, including boys from the New York City area. A small percentage of camp residents were girls. Regulations required camps to hold special permits from the New York Department of Health, but only one of every three did so.

Some 15 percent of cadets who chose living arrangements were city dwellers placed in remote rural areas that were far away from the farm work camps or day haul collection sites. In September 1943, farm cadets by the hundreds answered the call for labor. Hours of harvesting began with the truck ride at 6:00 a.m. and ended with a return trip at 6:00 p.m. The large number of cadets, up to eight hundred per selection site each day, led to an urgent appeal for women volunteers to serve as supervisors. Records on each cadet and farmer employer were kept. If either was not satisfied with the working or living arrangements, then transfers were quickly arranged.

Several boys replaced others in Niagara County, but not one was sent to Erie County, mostly because of the availability of day haul and migrant workers. Many of the living situations were mutually satisfactory, and many cadets returned to the same farm the following year. Occasionally, problems arose. Broken arms and legs, homesickness, problems in adjusting to farm life, illness, running away or, as one report described, "an affinity to possess other people's property," arose occasionally. Ultimately, 10 percent of the farmers were too impatient with inexperienced help, and another 5 percent were incapable of managing young people properly.

Most boys aged thirteen to seventeen were placed on farms as cadets during school summer vacations. To meet the harvest season labor shortage, New York State passed special legislation in late 1941 to release schoolchildren fourteen years of age and older for up to ten days of emergency harvesting without reducing state payments to the school districts. The school release plan was expanded to allow up to thirty days of release time for farm labor but limited work to fifteen days in any three-month period. Nearly forty thousand students harvested during the fall of 1941 on the school release plan. The agriculture program was part of feeding the Allies in the pre–Pearl Harbor era. During the spring, public schools registered students on enrollment cards requiring signed parental approval. Any child under sixteen was required to apply for work permits, but half of the students had no working papers. The Erie County War Council approached all sixty-seven Buffalo parochial schools for help, asking the principals to postpone the fall semester until the middle of September so that students might harvest crops. Critics wondered why it was necessary to interrupt educational activities for sixty thousand students when only seven or eight thousand were needed for the farms.

There were racial tensions on the farms as well. In the fall of 1943, a farmer refused to allow several black males from western New York to ride on his truck. The young men responded by pelting the farmer with ripe tomatoes. Later that day, two trucks for transporting volunteers to farmers were designated for blacks only. The federal agents responded to both violations by insisting the farmers would not be paid their share of federal money unless they treated black and white workers equally.

Women also were recruited for agriculture during the war. Requirements for the Woman's Land Army, an intensive farm labor program administered by the Department of Agriculture's extension service, were rigorous. Interested female residents of New York State from eighteen to forty years of age trained for four weeks in dairy, poultry and general farm work, and then they were placed as year-round workers. In keeping with the wartime mania for uniforms and insignia, Women's Land Army members wore official denim overalls, a cotton shirt and a jacket decorated with armbands and insignia. The four weeks of practical instruction concerned the care of farm animals, milking, handling horses, haying, tilling and harvesting, tractor driving, planting and fertilizing.

Each Land Army member thought of herself as "the woman behind the man behind the plow," a phrase that echoed the YWCA's "woman behind the man behind the gun" motto. The critical shortage had farmers recruiting relocated Japanese Americans, businessmen and furloughed servicemen as potential farmworkers. Few Japanese Americans were willing to work on farms, and even fewer farmers agreed to accept them. Conscientious objectors were assigned farm duties according to the location of the civilian public service camps, and furloughed servicemen mainly were used for short-term emergency harvesting situations. For example, five hundred naval trainees on loan from the Sampson Naval Training Station in the Finger Lakes region were assigned to western New York canning factories in the fall of 1943 to save the bean and corn crops.

Migrant labor had come under congressional scrutiny in 1940. Prior to the war, western New York farmers and canneries relied heavily on the 20,500 or so migrant farm labor workers who traveled the Atlantic coast throughout the year on trucks owned by crew leaders. They picked their way from Florida or the Carolinas to New York each year, working on subsistent wages and living in makeshift campsites provided by farmers. By 1943, the wartime gasoline rationing directives had reduced migrant travel dramatically, until a special agreement was struck to provide migrant worker trucks with gasoline. Government officials along the Atlantic coast, one of six identified migrant travel patterns, flagged down trucks at certain crossings to direct them to major farm sites. In 1943, New York State housed migrants in 330 farm labor camps; 50 were public, including 2 in Erie County and 1 in Niagara County. Erie and Niagara Counties contained 112 camps altogether.

Italian American and Polish American women who usually worked during peak cannery seasons continued to do so, sometimes lodging in cannery camps during the processing. Italian American families from Buffalo and Silver Creek rented rooms in town or in a tenement near the camp while their black counterparts lived in a tourist camp down the road. A packing plant in the Medina area that had lost 75 percent of its former employees to defense plants recruited women from the Tuscarora Indian reservation in Tonawanda and bused in 100 women from Akron, but only 20 percent of the usual Italian American women workers were available. They preferred defense work in the city. In Olean, over 150 Italian and Polish American housewives from Buffalo worked in the packing plant. Some of them had returned each year to work in the plant for the past fifteen to twenty years. The processing facilities' need for workers were so urgent that they persuaded several local industries to release workers temporarily for the peak processing season.

The Heinz Company ("57 Varieties") plant in the Medina area built up its workforce of cannery workers by employing a woman until she was "frozen" according to the USES's Buffalo Plan and then replacing her with another woman worker. But the replaced women were unable to secure regular employment or receive unemployment benefits, and that forced them to return to Heinz during the peak harvesting season for work. To be "frozen" meant that they did not get the certificate that would allow them either to receive unemployment insurance or to secure another defense job. In a preserving plant near Brockport, women workers were ordered to check out at the end of the day shift and work for one or two hours without pay.

The need for farm workers forced the agriculture business to call on new and untried labor sources. Agreements with the Caribbean islands of the Bahamas, Barbados and Jamaica as well as Mexico, Newfoundland and Canada permitted the recruitment of over 225,000 single men between 1942 and 1945 for farm labor. New York State requested 5,600 Jamaican laborers in 1943, but as of the midyear, only 1,250 had been placed. The largest group, 400 men, was sent to a farm labor camp in Brant, which had rich agricultural fields.

Acute unemployment in Jamaica because of wartime restriction on trade, especially bananas, led the United Fruit Company to recommend to the U.S. Department of Agriculture to utilize residents for farm labor. United Fruit recruited the men and initially placed them north of the Mason-Dixon line. Western New York residents' contact with the Jamaicans was rare, but the Buffalo Committee intervened when employee Victor Einach discovered the deplorable conditions of the Brant camp in 1943. Under his direction, the Jaycees provided a recreation program for the camp's residents. African Americans invited to a Jamaican recreational center were denied entry, which angered the Jamaicans.

The foreign nationals who worked out of the Brant camp traveled to western New York voluntarily, but in 1943, all the labor had been recruited, while shortage remained. One desperate processing plant wrote to the state director to request Italian prisoners of war and tried to persuade him to transfer the prisoners to his plant because many Italian Americans lived near the plant who could serve as interpreters. Governor Thomas Dewey ordered the use of western New York prisoners of war for agriculture, and eight hundred Italian POWs went to work in local tomato canning plants after Italy became a member of the Allies in 1943.

The German prisoners of war worked in the fields beginning in 1944. Over 4,500 of the 400,000 German prisoners of war held in the United States were moved to western New York and settled at fourteen locations in 1944. Fort Niagara was converted from an induction center in 1942 to the base camp for 1,000 prisoners in June 1944. The branch camps were Newark, Cobbs Hill, Dunkirk, Letchworth Park, Hamlin Beach, Oakfield, Medina, Attica, Sodus Point, Geneseo, Brockton, Marion and Naples. The encampments were in remote areas near agriculture and food processing plants. Some prisoners were housed in converted CCC camps, while others lived in the barracks constructed by food processing plants for their seasonal workers. Most of the German POWs were contracted to processing and canning factories despite protests by organized labor.

In compliance with the Geneva Convention, the POWs initially were paid 50 to 75 percent of the prevailing wage rates, which ranged from $0.45 to $0.55 per hour. Later, wage rates were set at $0.80 per hour. In 1944, an incentive payment plan allowed a POW to earn up to $1.20 per day. Working conditions were strictly controlled—no more than ten hours per day, including travel. The payment of canteen coupons equaled the salary of an American private in 1941, plus $0.10 per day for nonessentials. To secure a prisoner for labor, employers had to obtain certification that all other sources of farm labor were exhausted.

The initial interaction of approximately 3,200 newly arrived German POWs at Fort Niagara and residents was casual. Groups of prisoners wore shorts because uniform trousers had not arrived, and they waved to passersby. When not working in agriculture, the Germans occupied their time with sports, crafts, music, films and the library. Military intelligence carefully controlled available literature, emphasizing books and movies to educate the POWs about American democracy.

Only 8 percent of the prisoners knew English, so courses in the language were very popular. Internees included several divisions of the SS Panzers; however, the mixture of prisoners did not include devoted Nazis. Not all the prisoners were ethnic Germans; two hundred Russians wearing German uniforms were interned. The German POW program lasted from 1944 to 1946. Fort Niagara's camp population fluctuated as new prisoners arrived and others were returned to Germany. Socialization between prisoners and some residents appeared to be both tolerant and aloof, although national magazines expressed American fears that German POWs received better food and treatment than our citizens. Servicemen's families and returned veterans complained about the high wages their enemies received under civil conditions when they or friends had been treated badly in the German camps. The answer was that the Nazis would treat Americans worse if the United States did not follow the Geneva conventions. Special treatment from the German American community was not evident other than a German-speaking priest from nearby Stella Niagara, a convent of Franciscan sisters, serving the Catholic POWs along with three German-speaking ministers for the Protestant churchgoers. Thus, attendance at Fort Niagara's chapel was cited as the largest among all camps. The POWs passed through western New York with hardly a trace to recall their passing except the murals a prisoner painted at Fort Niagara.

6

THE CHILDREN'S WAR

Children and teenagers in Buffalo were not sheltered from the war. Joan Staley remembered, "My brother was drafted at eighteen in the Army Air Corps in 1942, and I don't remember when he returned. He served in France and D-day, possibly Normandy. Then he was sent to the Philippines." She was fourteen when the Japanese attacked Pearl Harbor.

Families worried about the safety of fathers, brothers, uncles, nephews—and daughters, nieces and aunts—and wondered when they would see them again. Historian Tuttle wrote of the emotional toll of single-parent families and of the stress of total war on children forced to grow up too soon. But teenagers, like adults, also enjoyed recreation. Staley related attending the movie theaters, roller skating and ice skating and taking the *Canadiana* with her girlfriends:

> *I first worked at the five and dime for fifteen cents an hour and then got a job at Dunlop Tire to make rubber and worked after school for fifty cents an hour. They* [the high school] *gave us more credits than we needed, and we were going to school half a day. Kenmore High School never graduated another class in January. I was sixteen when I started at Dunlop—1943 and 1944. I worked in the summer at Dunlop. I painted blimps and water targets and pulled them around. I wore coveralls in the factory like garage mechanics do, and it was very hot to dry the cement. I was very hot.*

Increasing numbers of young men and women entered the workplace before completing school or attempting to combine work and school. Teenagers provided the largest number of extra wartime workers. While teens remained in school longer during the Depression because graduation did not lead to employment, the wide variety of opportunities for unskilled labor during the war encouraged dropping out.

By 1944, over 2.1 million teens were employed—more than those normally expected in peacetime. In some regions of the country, 2 of every 3 teenagers dropped out of school. About 1 million nationwide left school early to take full-time employment or enlist, and 1.5 million carried a school-plus-job load by 1945.

In western New York, approximately two thousand students left high school by the fall of 1940 to work. Former mayor Jimmy Griffin was a high-school dropout. He quit South Park High School as a sophomore and went to work in the grain elevators during the war at age sixteen. After the war, he returned to school and graduated from Our Lady of Victory High School in Lackawanna in 1948.

Some boys dropped out of school to work until they were old enough for induction or enlistment. As the war continued and seventeen-year-olds were sought, the armed forces actively sought out high school boys for specialized training. Kenmore High School was one of many that offered accelerated work-study programs.

"I graduated at age seventeen," said Joan Staley, "and they wouldn't take me at Chevy because you had to be eighteen. So, I worked for a woman who owned a girls' camp in Allegheny as a secretary until I was eighteen. I returned to Dunlop and worked in the office until I was married."

In late 1944 and 1945, the federal and state governments pushed a back-to-school program. They wanted to remove mostly unskilled employees from the workforce so that adults could take those jobs. Half of those in domestic service, such as maids, babysitters and housekeepers, were teenaged girls. Many left for retail work for better pay. The back-to-school program primarily applied to teens in retail and restaurant positions that their elders had abandoned to take skilled defense jobs.

Before the war, agriculture employed the greatest number of teenagers. But agriculture was notorious for minimal child safety laws, permitting longer workdays, truancy and hazardous conditions. Many farm families moved into urban areas after 1942 to seek more lucrative employment and did not return to farming.

Although economists concerned themselves with reducing causes of postwar unemployment, parents feared most that their children, now with some money in their pockets, would turn into juvenile delinquents. The federal Children's Bureau pronounced with authority that delinquency in wartime was caused by a craving for adventure, the entry of mothers into industry and the adoration young girls had for soldiers and sailors.

The song "You Can't Say 'No' to a Soldier" seemed to apply to every girl who took a second look at a young man in uniform. But child educators complained that the numbers of petty thefts, gang wars and sexual offenses were rising, although police statistics did not agree. Wartime stresses exacerbated juvenile crime, warned the Children's Bureau, as parental guidance and supervision was lacking in homes where the father was a member of the armed services and the mother was employed.

Victory girls, Good-time Charlottes or uniform-happy "khaki wackies," as teenaged female camp followers were called, lingered near military camps or recreational areas frequented by servicemen. Most of the men in their age group had been drafted or enlisted in the armed forces. During the war, western New York communities experienced the full variety of delinquent behavior. "I was only trying to give this fellow a good time on furlough. I don't know when he might be shot or wounded," said a fifteen-year-old girl. "After all, us junior high school girls would like to do her (*sic*) bit in the war, too!"

During World War I, the Boy Scouts, Girl Scouts, YMCA and YWCA were relatively new organizations that provide activities and affiliations for children feeling adrift in a chaotic world. Although those clubs were still around in the 1940s, their focus was on war work, not on having fun.

Delinquent children in Erie County ended up in Children's Court, referred by parents, school and social agencies. The Buffalo Police Department established a youth crime prevention bureau in 1938. Over 3,500 cases were handled by the bureau in 1943, and less than 20 percent of those were referred to Children's Court. The youth crime prevention bureau of the 1940s was much like the police athletic league of the 1960s, a means of letting youngsters know that police were their friends. Shared activities between young people and police officers were supposed to build rapport and discourage potential criminal behavior. Bureau officials could deal with delinquents in ways that would not appear in official records. They could notify parents or refer the child to the appropriate agency.

What caused delinquency? Better ask what didn't cause delinquency. Some answered the war, older peers, parental neglect, radio and magazines, mass culture, pulp novels, comics and lowering of religious standards. In 1943, a Buffalo city judge declared the urgent need for a 10:00 p.m. curfew for all children under sixteen years old. He stated that parental neglect allowed children to run around the streets in search of trouble. Some fourteen- or fifteen-year-old boys led gangs of children as young as seven years old, the judge claimed. Child neglect cases before Children's Court peaked in 1944. Most of the neglected children were younger than seven years of age; however, the delinquents were teens.

Many adults found delinquency to be a symptom of how disturbing the war was to youngsters, and the Family Service Society focused on the terrible effects of family disintegration. The Buffalo Superintendent of Schools blamed the mandatory staggered hours for war factories for encouraging delinquency and dropouts. To manage shift traffic and conserve public transportation, the starting time for high schools had been reset from 9:00 a.m. to 9:45 a.m. Gang warfare, vandalism and the victory girl phenomenon received the most publicity in the community and thus were the most visible marks of juvenile delinquency.

Buffalo had a history of youth gangs, and the trend continued through the 1930s with the Georgian Boys, Vigilantes, the Screws and others. Boys' clubs were established in 1933 to provide a wholesome atmosphere. In 1943, the city was shaken by a gang war between Jewish and Christian boys in a very good neighborhood—although the conflict was more ethnic than religious in nature. Tensions were heightened when a Jewish youth was beaten by four Christian boys—two Catholic and two Protestant—who were arrested for the assault. The conflict peaked with an all-out fight of one hundred boys, some brandishing knives and clubs, the others flashing zip guns. The Italian Catholic students sided with the Jewish gang against the Irish Protestant youngsters. Religious leaders organized a meeting, and the participants settled their differences amicably.

A wave of vandalism in 1943 alarmed residents in Buffalo and the suburbs. Residential and commercial properties were damaged. Smashed streetlights, seats and fixtures in movie theaters; shattered windowpanes; desecrated cemeteries; and diverted electric trolleys kept the police busy. Gangs terrorized certain low-income housing projects and overcrowded city wards. Prompted by neighborhood patrols by veterans, extra police protection, raids and educational programs, 130 delinquent boys were charged with burglary or unlawful entry, while half of the girls involved were defined as ungovernable. Most of the children were aged thirteen to fifteen years old. Older girls were more likely to be sent to a psychiatrist for running away or having sex.

During World War I, more servicemen were out of action because of syphilis and gonorrhea than in combat. The victory girls were considered teenage menaces representing unnecessary casualties of war. "Prostitution was an Axis [i.e., enemy] partner" said public health advocates, and a menace to the health and efficiency of the army and navy. At mobilization sites across the country, sexually transmitted disease rates had risen a great deal since the trainees arrived. Some public health physicians suggested that all women employees at restaurants and bars near encampments be registered and tested for syphilis before new troops arrived.

Among the prostitutes were juvenile delinquents. Some girls turned to prostitution as a last resort because they needed money. The YWCA put on a play describing the adventure of a victory girl named Silly Sally Sue as a warning:

Sally Sue was a very pretty girl with a very little brain.
Sally wanted to do something for the soldiers
And the sailors
And the Marines
To say nothing of the Air Corps.
They were very handsome
With a snappy uniform.
After all, they were going away
To fight for their country,
And for Sally Sue—she was sure of that.

Buffalo was long known to be a haven for prostitution during the 1920s, with over one hundred brothels in the red-light district and at least as many outside the area. Investigators visiting in 1928 at the request of Buffalo's Committee of Sixteen exposed the friendly commercial benefits and social relations between the brothels and the city fathers. A flurry of activity in 1931 temporarily reduced what was considered disorderly behavior, but a changeover of police chiefs and judges allowed prostitution to reestablish itself. Fort Niagara's major induction center in nearby Lewiston flooded Niagara Falls and Buffalo with bored and anxious young soldiers ready to kick up their heels before being sent for military training. Because of the proximity to the Canadian border, call girls from Ontario and Québec flocked to the area.

Niagara Falls boasted of brothels with names like James Thornton's Café, Sugar's Place, Tuckers and Ernie Wilsons. Entering the United States

ONE PIECE | ONE PIECE | ONE PIECE | ONE PIECE | ONE PIECE

IN ORDER TO CONSERVE MAN POWER FOR VITAL WAR INDUSTRIES and PREVENT HOARDING

NOOKEY RATION CARD No. 000606

For Fiscal Year Ending July 1, 1944

In accepting this card, the holder agrees to abide by all Rules and Regulations issued by the Federal Administrator

Name.......
Address.......
Race.......Age.......Height.......
Color of Eyes.......Color of Hair.......
Married or Single.......Complexion.......

— WARNING !! —
Be sure you have complied with all the Federal Regulations before Tearing Off a Piece

ONE PIECE | ONE PIECE | ONE PIECE | ONE PIECE | ONE PIECE

Everything was rationed. *Author's collection.*

by one of the bridges crossing the Niagara River or cross-linking Ontario to Sodus and then traveling through Niagara Falls, enterprising Canadian prostitutes set up housekeeping during the war. If arrested, they were deported under the little-known Bennett Act, which prohibited the transfer of foreign nationals for immoral purposes. Female runaway cases evoked fears of the Mann Act of 1910 against white slavery, the transportation of women over state boundaries for immoral purposes. In 1942, two teenage Buffalo girls were picked up for soliciting by Springville, Massachusetts police. After arriving in New York, the fourteen- and fifteen-year-old girls were hired by a magazine subscription company to visit defense areas to sell orders. The Department of Labor stated that although the young people had crossed state lines, the companies could not be prosecuted because selling subscriptions was not immoral. During the same year, the Buffalo police commissioner reorganized and expanded the vice squad, focusing on the reduction of commercialized prostitution, and arrests for vice dropped by 60 percent between 1942 and 1944.

An anti-vice campaign launched in Niagara Falls, another haven for prostitution, netted ten Buffalo girls, seven of whom were teenaged victory girls. The young women were treated for sexually transmitted diseases whether they had them or not. New cases of syphilis and gonorrhea among the servicemen peaked in 1943 and 1944 as Fort Niagara switched from induction center to prisoner-of-war camp headquarters, but gradually decreased until the war ended.

7

GROWING PAINS

During the war emergency, utility services, recreational programs and physical facilities expanded to accommodate new defense workers. Lured by the promise of defense jobs, ten thousand newcomers needed more than five thousand apartments. The occupancy rate of existing housing was 100 percent. "The city of Good Neighbors is appropriate," a newcomer observed, "but it sure is crowded!" War contractors feared that not enough housing would turn away additional workers. Conditions found in World War I, such as overcrowding and sky-high rent, were the major obstacles.

Despite the loss of thousands of residents to the armed forces, newcomers for defense employment soon found housing hard to find in overcrowded western New York. At the peak of migration in mid-1943, seventy thousand individuals had moved into the area. As during World War, I, active recruitment in the South brought many African Americans to the area, aggravating an already critical housing situation. In 1940, the population was eighteen thousand, and the black population increased to twenty-five thousand in 1943. Increased visibility of minority groups multiplied tension, and some residents simply disliked all newcomers, especially resenting the influx of war workers from outside the state.

Existing housing was filled first, after extensive room registration drives to maximize the use of current vacancies. The Erie County homeless registration in 1941 kept records of unoccupied rooms, apartments and houses and directed renters to landlords. By 1943, 120 newcomers and

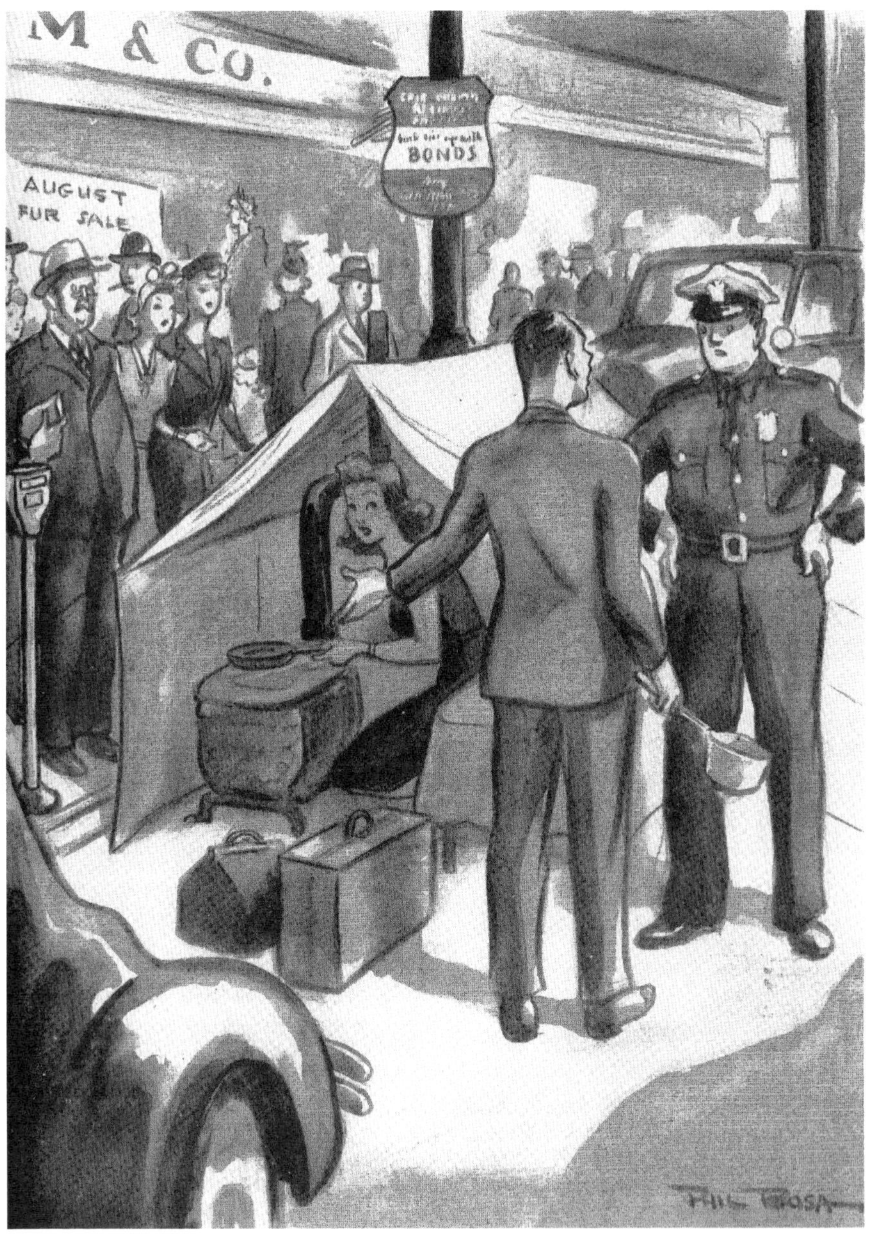

Buffalo Business, October 1942. *Reproduction by permission of the Buffalo & Erie County Public Library, Buffalo, New York.*

180 local citizens who were relocating from the country or from a suburb utilized the service weekly. A "repair for defense" campaign converted 7,500 dwellings to defense housing and provided additional rental space for newcomers. None of the housing was inspected, so renting apartments was "buyer beware." During World War I, severe housing shortages led to frequent labor turnovers and canceled contracts, a situation Buffalo wanted to avoid. In July 1941, the state surveyed thirty-three population centers, and Buffalo was the most seriously affected, requiring immediate action. The federal defense housing coordinator ordered 15,000 units for immediate construction.

New defense plants were frequently established in areas outside the cities, locations that were off regular transportation routes and outside of existing housing. It was soon evident the new construction was necessary to attract and retain the workers for required war production. Federal legislation in 1940 provided funding for certain types of war housing and related community facilities, such as water systems, sewage, schools, hospital centers and childcare centers. Slum clearance was a secondary purpose of defense housing, as seven hundred family units were demolished between 1940 and 1943. Since most of the new housing was placed in suburbs, the secondary objective was mostly unfulfilled. The map of blighted areas in Buffalo traced the familiar small set of streets set aside for African American housing. Black residents were limited to two small residential areas ("black belt") on the east side of Buffalo: Cold Springs, a neighborhood bounded by East Ferry and East Delavan, and Masten Park, a neighborhood centering on Best Street from Michigan to Jefferson Avenue and abutting Cold Springs. Crime rates and tuberculosis cases were highest in these areas, while educational and recreational facilities were minimal.

Buffalo had begun a slum clearance program during the Great Depression, replacing substandard housing with flats. The first project was Kenfield, completed in 1937, with 50 experimental low-rent developments and 650 apartments. Kenfield was a federal housing project out of the Buffalo Municipal Housing Association's jurisdiction, yet blacks were banned from occupancy.

Discouraged but not disheartened, the local National Union League chapter, which advocated for African American rights, turned its efforts to projects in other areas of the city. Three neighborhoods were affected: black neighborhood Bullard Park; one identified as Italian, Lakeview; and the third as Irish Catholic, Commodore Perry. The Buffalo and National Union League disagreed with the site chosen for Willard Park, because the area was not sufficiently large and its proximity to an iron foundry and substandard housing was undesirable.

The Buffalo Municipal Housing Authority (BMHA) countered that the small number of units was due to the difficulty of finding sufficient number of black families to qualify as tenants. Only the Willard Park project accepted black residents. All three projects were still under construction in 1940 when the newcomer war workers began to arrive. Housing outside the city was no better. In Lackawanna, Bethlehem Steel built 400 company houses for white emloyees, forcing many black employees to find housing in the already overcrowded Buffalo black belt. The Baker homes project of 256 units opened in 1938, and at first, blacks were not allowed as tenants.

Defense housing could be temporary or permanent. Temporary housing included trailers and prefabricated units of barracks or other simplified dwellings. These were found near war plants outside the city where affordable housing was scarce. Permanent housing was more elaborate, of different sized apartments, attached single-family homes or duplexes. City planners attempted to establish the permanent projects as self-sufficient communities, as they were usually situated in areas without services.

Two defense housing projects were planned to relieve the requirement for convenient housing for African Americans: LaSalle Courts (206 units) and Langfield Homes (594 units). These were fully occupied by 1941. In 1942, racial tensions reached new heights when a federal official announced the possibility of reserving LaSalle Courts for blacks who worked in North Buffalo defense industries. A race relations mediator was dispatched by the federal Public Housing Authority to disallow segregated housing but promised that 200 of the proposed 1,000 units would be set aside for blacks. But the result was that no black tenants were permitted to sell their houses, and housing officials were forced to search for another site. They recommended a South Buffalo site, which provoked strong organized resistance from the residents. The next several attempts of providing public defense housing for blacks met with failure due to angry Irish Catholics organized by several local priests. Polish Americans stated their objection was to the idea of public housing, but what they meant was not wanting black housing in their neighborhood. In fact, the Buffalo Chamber of Commerce even visited Washington, D.C., to protest the establishment of public defense housing. Left with the small extension to Willard Park Courts, Buffalo blacks were discouraged about the possibility of securing decent low-income housing in any other parts of the city. This situation led to limited job opportunities, as the buses and streetcars did not reach low-income areas.

Over twelve thousand new dwelling units were made available in Buffalo between April 1940 and March 1943, but the housing shortage continued. For blacks, it was unbearable. In 1944, a survey of thirty-two blocks in the black belt revealed that 2,300 black families and 650 individuals were crammed into two thousand units. Overcrowding was so bad that people slept in rooms on shifts or spent the night in cars.

The Buffalo Commission on Defense and Employment continued to collect data on housing for blacks in western New York during the war. They interviewed members of the BMHA, who said that Buffalo was not ready for integration just yet. Besides, they had not deliberately set segregationist policy for housing projects—it just happened that way. They complained that blacks did not apply for projects that would reject their applications, just as they did not apply for employment in industries that refused to hire them. The BMHA director, J. Clagett, claimed that the situation was the fault of blacks because they did not want to live apart from their neighborhoods and claimed that on a per capita basis, African Americans were getting a better opportunity in public housing than non-whites. This statement was based entirely in fiction, since black tenants paid higher rents than others using private or public housing.

The Buffalo Committee found that blacks and whites lived in peaceful unity in the two existing housing projects. Buffalo and Lackawanna had employees who worked together at the steel plants until the war, when white tenants began objecting to blacks. Five black ministers petitioned the Lackawanna housing manager for an exclusively black project. This was odd and upset both blacks and whites, who were afraid they had to move for this to occur, but the Federal Housing Authority ignored the petition. Niagara Falls public housing also was integrated to some extent—what Buffalo Committee employee Victor Einach called "segregated in mixed occupancy"—since blacks lived at the same project as whites but blocks away from their white neighbors. Despite continued pressure on the municipal housing authorities, the Buffalo commission couldn't change housing patterns, and the labor unions did not intervene.

The major Buffalo private real estate developers pooled their resources and constructed residential housing in the suburbs. These were single-family homes and apartments to be sold in the early postwar era. A Catholic priest in Orchard Park coordinated the construction of one thousand garden homes, small homes with one-acre plots for growing vegetable gardens, planned for the express needs of industrial workers. The American Garden Homes Foundation was located near defense plants and in Lackawanna.

The CIO advertised a plan to build fifty low-cost homes for workers to live at the city's boundaries.

Between 1940 and 1944, over 14,600 dwellings were built for $45 million. Buffalo constructed 1,140 new publicly funded family dwellings, Niagara Falls over 2,500, Lackawanna 240, and North Tonawanda 50. In comparison, New York City had 1,900 new units. Western New York acquired more public housing than any other region in the state.

Some of the defense housing sites were planned as total communities. One was Cheektowaga's planned community of 1,050 units; it had parks, recreation areas and a shopping center. The community was called Ti-O-Run-Da. In 1947, residents purchased homes at this popular site when the government divested itself of the property. Just north of Buffalo, the Town of Tonawanda received federal money for the 1,200-unit community project called Sheridan-Parkside. This project was next to a railroad track near the Niagara River, and was a group of poorly constructed dwellings in the industrial portion of town. The magazine *American Builder* called Sheridan-Parkside "pneumonia flats." The project suffered from numerous delays, resulting in hasty construction. Without basements, the houses collected water. The local fire department claimed that the project was a fire hazard because fire hoses did not fit on the hydrants. With its cracked pavement, botched ductwork, a small-sized incinerator and demoralizing landscape, Sheridan-Parkside did not attract many residents until the war ended. Lackawanna acquired two defense projects totaling 600 units: Ridgewood Village and Albright Court. The state also funded North Tonawanda's 200-unit and Tonawanda's 150-unit Colin Kelly Heights, named after a war hero. (Kelly was the first American B-17 pilot to be shot down in combat after Pearl Harbor.)

Niagara Falls received more defense housing than all the rest put together: 3,900 units, of which 300 were state-funded and the rest federally funded. Hennepin Manor had 150 units, Packard Court had 166 units, Griffin Center Court had 134 units, Pine Acres had 1,700 units and the immense Griffin Manor had 3,150 units. None of these was fully or even substantially occupied, a situation explained best by the relative lack of public transportation between Niagara Falls housing and the war plants in Buffalo and the suburbs. By February 1944, only 50 of Pine Acres' 1,700 units and 50 of Hyde Park's 600 units were occupied. Both defense projects were integrated. This may have been unappealing to some groups.

After less than two years of use, Hennepin Manor's 150 single homes were up for sale. Because of the temporary nature of 2,700 units, most of the

Niagara Falls federal housing ghost towns were pulled down or moved to other locations at war's and. For example, the government of France bid on Pine Acres units. Bewildered Niagara frontier residents must have watched the dismantling of the temporary defense housing with dismay, since the units were of better quality than most of the permanent accommodations where they lived.

Living in defense housing was no more dangerous than living in permanent residences. Calls for domestic violence, petty theft and vice occupied the police. But on August 4, 1944, all eyes were on Pine Acres in Niagara Falls. The New York State Police Bureau of Criminal Investigation handled the case.

At 5:00 a.m., Mr. and Mrs. Joseph Raybon were sleeping in their apartment when Mrs. Raybon awoke, convinced there was an intruder in the bedroom. To quote from the police report, "Before she had time to ward off this mysterious person whom she believed to be a negro, the man began choking her." With her scream, he jumped out the window, and the police were notified. They found no one.

About forty-five minutes later, Mr. Alvie Kennedy came home from working the night shift at Bell Aircraft. His house was one block from the first attack. His three young children were crying. In the bedroom, his young wife, Miriam, was "out-stretched on the floor, raped and murdered." Police believed that the same man was involved in both cases. The eight-year-old Kennedy son heard his mother screaming and ran into her bedroom. The attacker tossed him into another bedroom and began strangling him. When Mr. Kennedy knocked on the door after returning from work, the man left by the back window. Young Jimmy described him as "dark, no clothes, black hair."

Neighbors recalled a similar attack from February of the same year in an apartment close to the first attack. Mrs. Dorothea Newgarden, assaulted and strangled, was found dead. Could this be a serial killer?

The Pine Acres murders brought carloads of onlookers to gawk at the place where the murders took place. One portion of Pine Acres was a state-funded integrated public housing project of 300 apartments divided into 175 for whites and 125 for blacks several blocks away. Detectives searched carefully to find "a pair of Cooper's Jockey shorts, size 30, a pocket knife, a handkerchief, a pubic hair of the Negroid race, and…a portion of a palm print." None of these belonged to Mr. Kennedy.

The police took the fingerprint and palm prints of every male resident in the project and asked where they had been when the attacks happened. The partial palm prints of Robert Barnes, a black resident living a few blocks from the Kennedy home, turned up positive. He initially cooperated with the police, although when he was arrested, he was wearing a pair of jockey shorts just like those found at the scene but with the label removed. Barnes confessed, and then took back his statement and was given a lie-detector test. The police said that he had chewed a hole in the instrument's hose to change its response so it would prove his innocence.

A local CIO representative and a group of Communist Party members took up Barnes's case, claiming that he had been drugged and beaten into making a confession. The Communist Party of the USA's platform encouraged better race relations. Even Buffalo Committee employee Victor Einach was followed by the FBI as a Communist sympathizer, which he was not.

At first, the police denied they had mistreated Barnes. Then they agreed that the injuries to the arrested black man had occurred in self-defense. The Crime Bureau identified the alleged offender only by a palm print, which was a form of evidence used in New York courts but only once before, during World War I. Despite questions about the validity of this evidence, the court found Barnes guilty and sentenced him to life imprisonment at Attica. Three attacks and two murders in an integrated and sparsely settled defense housing distressed neighbors, which may have been one reason the development had few tenants compared to its size.

The new defense industries and housing developments taxed western New York's already inadequate infrastructure. Basic needs for water and sewers, hospital facilities, schools and other urban services were not being met. Ten water systems served the area, drawing 80 percent of the supply from Lake Erie. But distribution of water to new areas became insufficient for supply needs. The federal government paid for new interconnections, a storage reservoir and feeder mains in Niagara Falls, Tonawanda and Buffalo specifically for defense housing projects, the Bell plants and other defense industries.

In 1941, overcrowded hospital and medical facilities were a concern. In 1942, the occupancy rate for hospitals was over 90 percent. Federal funds added thirty hospital beds—far fewer than were needed. Erie County sent three hundred doctors to war, one-third of all doctors in the area. The medical school at the University of Buffalo was on an accelerated plan to turn out doctors in three years and produce premed majors in sixteen months to produce sixty to eighty doctors yearly. But the medical school professors were already on double and triple load. The public health department worried about the possibility of smallpox outbreaks like the one in Pennsylvania. Due to the serious shortage of nurses—thousands enrolled in the army and the navy—the federal government enabled three local hospitals to expand their student nurse training facilities. More schools were needed, and at Niagara Falls, Tonawanda and Cheektowaga, enrollment increased 50 percent over capacity.

Despite the arrival of newcomers throughout the war, western New York's total population did not increase dramatically. In 1940, western New York, including the cities of Buffalo and Niagara Falls, had a population of 947,000, of which most lived in Buffalo. By 1946, when most of the veterans had returned, the city's population was over 870,000, a small increase from the prewar level in the suburbs between Buffalo and Niagara Falls along the industrial corridor, where most of the new residents resided. Three-quarters of the suburban population lived between Buffalo and Niagara Falls, while both cities' populations changed little.

When veterans returned, the wartime housing situation reached critical levels. The Buffalo City Council held hearings on veterans' housing, and veterans and their families were surveyed through a local newspaper. Over 3,500 veterans applied for housing in April 1946. Several public housing projects were converted to low-income facilities, while others began to limit new applicants to veteran families. And in Tonawanda, Sheridan Parkside's occupation rate increased from 600 units to 1,100 units in July 1946.

The governor promised 500 more housing units for western New York. City schools were converted into apartments, and barracks for military installations were temporarily relocated on Grand Island and in state parks. Residents offered summer cottages along the lake to homeless veterans. Fort Niagara entered a third phase of existence, from induction center for drafted men to base camp for prisoners of war to remodeled apartments for veterans. Old St. Mary's asylum and infant home was turned into veteran apartments by the state in 1947. Despite the urgent need for housing, the chamber of commerce continued to resist public housing. At the end of 1947, six local banks refused to back municipally subsidized public housing despite the city's offer to provide land and remit taxes. The majority of the twenty-four thousand single homes developed between 1940 and 1948 were built in self-contained suburban communities with new shopping malls, schools and libraries.

For some veterans, the postwar era brought the development of a new community. The Veterans Project, a neighborhood of army barracks brought to the Kensington-Fillmore, gave young families the sense of becoming part of an extended family. These small units backed up to a dump site near what today is part of the Erie County Medical Center. Famed children's author and illustrator Lois Lenski based her book *Project Boy* (1954) on the Veterans Project. Millie Zimmerman told a *Buffalo News* reporter about the housing: "The walls were thin and the rooms were drafty, but I was so happy to be with my family in my own little place."

8

FOR THE DURATION

The enduring image of World War II is the raising of the flag on Mount Suribachi in Iwo Jima. This famous photograph by Joe Rosenthal has been translated into statues placed at memorial sites around the country. A Buffalonian was there for the photo, and here is his story, as related by his son Timothy McCarthy.

Edward James McCarthy served as a pharmacy mate in the U.S. Navy. During the invasion of Iwo Jima, he was aboard the USS *Fondulac*. On February 23, 1945, McCarthy was present for the raising of the American flag on Mount Suribachi, a volcano on the eight-square-mile hell known as the island of Iwo Jima.

The invasion of Iwo Jima lasted from February 19 to March 26, 1945, a ferocious Marine battle in which the American casualties (26,000) exceeded the Japanese (22,000). Almost 6,800 U.S. servicemen were killed.

While the fighting for Mount Suribachi was still going on, six marines struggled to raise the flag near the the top of the volcano. Those on the invasion ship saw this act of defiance and cheered wildly. The commander of the invasion fleet saw this as morale building and ordered that a larger flag be put up to replace the smaller U.S. flag that was raised. Photographs of both events were taken.

Joe Rosenthal of the Associated Press took the famous photo of the flag-raising event. Marine photographer Robert Campbell captured several men taking down the small flag while in the background the larger one was raised.

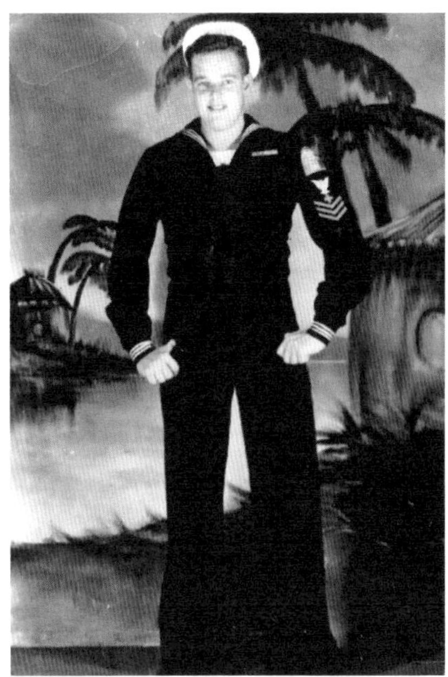

Edward McCarthy (navy). *Collection of Timothy McCarthy.*

As relayed by his wife, Kitty McCarthy, Edward McCarthy picked up two copies of the prints from the original negative of that event. The photographer, assumed to be Rosenthal, said it was to become a famous photo of the invasion and maybe of World War II.

The two copies of the first flag-raising show flak in the sky from artillery and large naval guns—which do not appear in the second event. The marines raising the second flag—the large one—were sent back to the states for touring. The whereabouts of the first flag, the smaller flag, is not known; a marine near the site folded it to keep the flag safe but must have lost it.

Although men in the armed forces, whether enlisted or drafted, were called to serve "for the duration" of the war, several unlucky souls also were assigned to the Japanese or German occupation. One was my uncle, Arnold Dold, who was drafted in 1944 near the end of the war and ended up in Germany after V-E Day to help with the occupation. He spoke of the destruction of the land and the desperation of the civilians.

Pilots and air crew kept flight logs. Buffalonian William J. Gibson's log was not just a listing of places and flying time but his emotions during time of war.

Gibson was born in Scotland in 1919 and naturalized in 1924. He was a radio operator in the Army Air Corps and his total flying hours in B-24s were 484.15 in sixty-seven flights. His last World War II flight was on May 22, 1945, from England to the United States.

More B-24s were built than any other American airplane. It edged out the B-17 on most performance criteria (speed, range, bomb load). Its crewmen claimed 2,600 enemy aircraft shot down. The B-24 design was simple, and the fuel consumption was highly efficient, although the narrow interior due to the positioning of the bomb racks limited movement within the aircraft, which led to the nickname the "Flying Coffins." American B-24 bombers

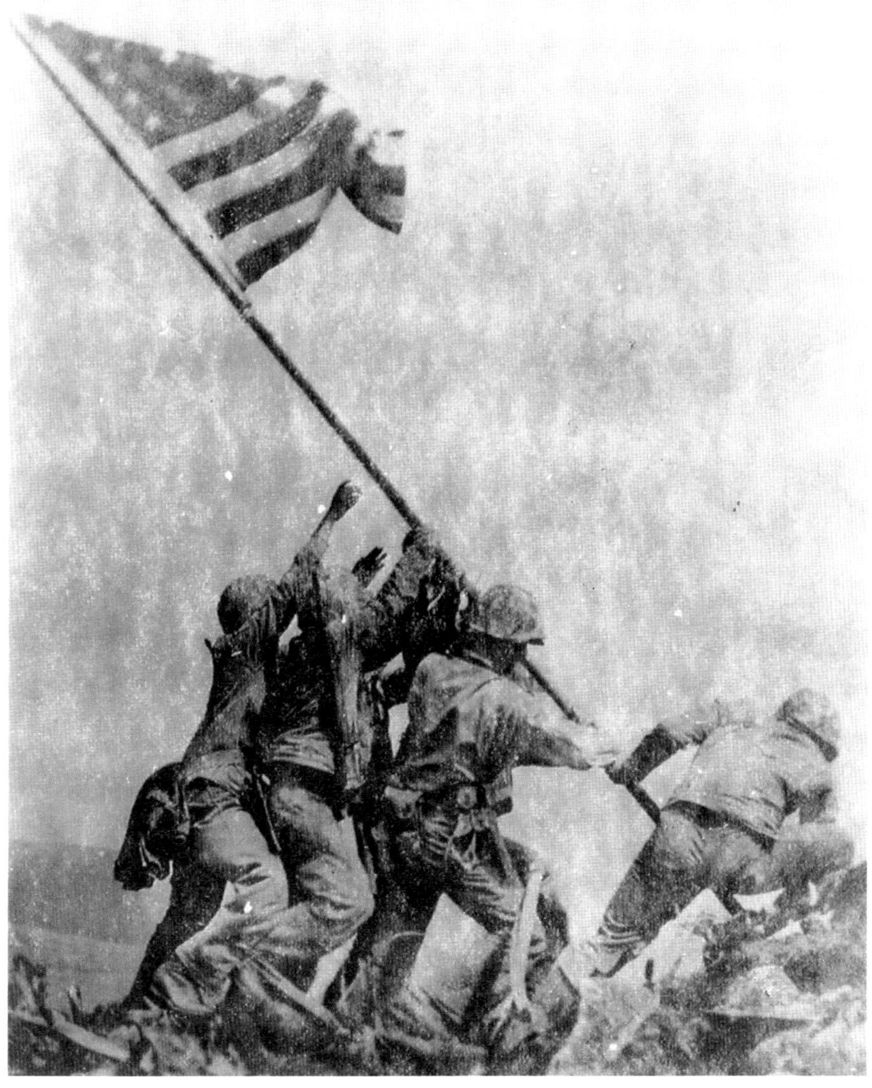

Iwo Jima flag photo with flak on battlefield, given to Edward McCarthy, February 23, 1945. *Collection of Timothy McCarthy.*

attacked the Romanian oilfields at Ploiesti and later made a return visit to the same target during Operation Tidal Wave in August 1943.

By the end of the war, a stunning 18,482 aircraft were built, making them the most produced Allied aircraft in the war. They were used by every Allied service in every theater; 2,100 of them served with the British, 1,200 with the

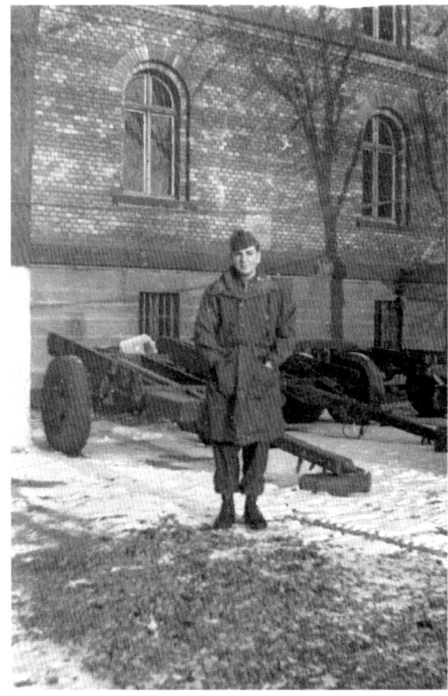

Arnold Dold (army) in occupied Germany. *Collection of Rosemary Dold.*

Canadians and 287 with the Australians. A few served in the Mediterranean Sea with the South Africans, while the majority were the property of the American forces.

The specifications made them the ultimate war machine: 10 by 12.7 millimeter Browning M2 machine guns, bomb load of 1,200 kilograms for very long-range missions, 2,300 kilograms for long range and 3,600 kilograms for short range. The B-24 ran on a crew of eleven. The radio operator also was a gunner. The B-24 had the radio table and equipment just aft of the flight deck, ahead of the bomb bay.

Radio operator William J. Gibson recorded details of thirty of the sixty-seven flights he made on a B-24, aka "Flying Boxcar." His plane bombed the Minden (Germany) Aqueduct on December 6, 1944, and the railroad yards at Hanau (Germany) on December 12, 1944, where two B-24s went down over the target. Gibson wrote about the date, time, target, flak level and whether fighters were in the area. (Flak is antiaircraft fire.) His crew knocked out bridges (Coblenz) and the Goering tank factory at Magdeburg, Germany, where they were forced to land near Paris. Gibson took the opportunity to see London, Berlin and Paris within twenty-four hours. Here are his personal notes exactly as written in the log. The juxtaposition of log details and Gibson's comments is revealing:

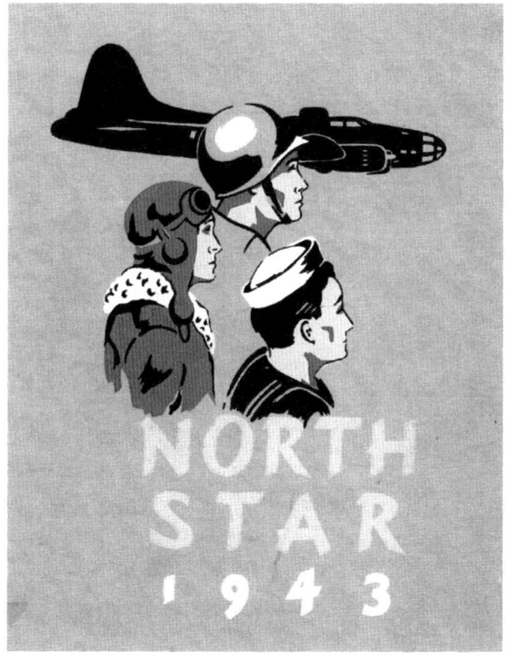

North Star 1943. *McClelland Barclay, USNR, 1943.*

2.23.44 Paderborn, Germany—briefed for low level [flying] *but weather was so bad at times we couldn't see the wing tips* [sweated].
2.25.44 Jet airfield at Giebelstadt despite intense flak, had visual target, and we really wiped it out.
2.26.44 Berlin—Flak was moderate—cloud cover. Spent half an hour alone in the bomb bay getting door closed. It was 50 degrees below but I sweat plenty. Lost chute over target.

4.25.45 Jarteburg, Austria. Flew over Alps on way out saw Hitler's hideout smoking where RAF [Royal Air Force—England] *hit. Flak was moderate but they were tracking us! Boys flying next to our ship said they were sure we "had it." Fooled them again. No holes.*

Gibson was demobilized on October 13, 1945, in Tucson, and lived a long life. He was one of the lucky ones.

Not all combatants were so fortunate. Families all over the city displaying the symbol of a son or husband in service dreaded the arrival of a Western Union messenger. The telegram announcing the casualty of a serviceman read: "The Secretary of War desires me to express regret on the loss of your son John Doe killed in action March 8, 1945. Letter to follow." A similar form was used to notify the family of a loved one wounded in action, missing in action or taken prisoner. And sometimes the telegrams were wrong.

On January 2, 1943, three Buffalo families were told their sons had become Japanese prisoners in the Philippines after Americans reluctantly surrendered at the battle of Corregidor. Second Lieutenant Robert J. Huffcut was the son of the attendance supervisor of the Buffalo Board of Education. He had accepted his army commission from General MacArthur and had been secretary to High Commissioner of the Philippines, Francis Sayre.

The POW families sought any sign that their sons were alive. Huffcut's father asked the Reverend Pacifico A. Ortiz, SJ, who came to Canisius High School if he had seen his son. The priest had slept in the same tunnel with him for two months. Ortiz was the personal chaplain to Philippine president Manuel Quezon.

There was an ironic twist of fate to this story. Huffcutt graduated from School 60, Riverside High School, and Cornell University, class of 1934. He was nominated for the Scalp and Blade Scholarship. The other nominee, who won the award, was Herbert F.K. Bahr, who graduated from Technical High School. While Huffcut suffered in a POW camp, Bahr had been sent to federal jail in Atlanta, Georgia, serving a thirty-year term on charges of conspiracy to spy for the Nazis. He was convicted in August 1942. Huffcutt was a hero, Bahr a traitor.

Author Hampton Sides wrote about the "The Great Raid" led by the U.S. Army Sixth Rangers on the notorious Cabanautan POW camp in the Philippines. Robert Huffcut was a survivor of the Battle of Corregidor, in which the Japanese made their final push to conquer the Philippines. He was picking eggplants in the camp garden when a Japanese guard, unprovoked, shot him in the arm. The other American soldiers begged the guard to let them care for him. The guard, nicknamed Liver Lips by the POWs, shot Huffcut in the head on August 11, 1944. By the time the Japanese commander allowed the Americans to tend to him, Huffcut was dead. The Japanese claimed that Huffcut had tried to escape. Months later, the U.S. Rangers and their allies liberated the camp's inhabitants. Huffcut's brother James lived in Tonawanda.

The second POW was Lieutenant Albert Chestnut, age twenty-three, supply officer with the U.S. Army Air Corps. He was wounded in action on December 8, 1941, when the Japanese attacked Clark Field at Pearl Harbor. Chestnut was a reserve officer called to active service in August 1941 in the Philippines. He was a mining engineer. Chestnut, according to *Buffalo News* reporter Brian Meyer, was from a well-off family in Buffalo.

He attended Nichols School ('35) and earned a degree in engineering from the Massachusetts Institute of Technology in 1939. Like many college men of his generation, he was a member of the U.S. Army Reserve Officers Training Corps. Six months before the Japanese attack on Pearl Harbor, he was called into active duty and given the rank of first lieutenant. Along with hundreds of other American soldiers, he became a POW when the Philippines fell to Japan and was sent to Osaka Main Camp Chikko near Osaka, Japan, where 4,123 other American POWs were held. Chestnut's capture was first reported to the International Committee of the Red Cross on May 7, 1942, and the last report was made on October 28, 1945. Based on these two reports, Albert was imprisoned for at least 1,270 days (over three years), one of the longest durations of captivity recorded. He endured the Bataan Death March and wrote in a tiny notebook about surviving the horrors of Japanese prison camps. The Buffalo History Museum cares for the fragile volumes now. In the postwar era, Chestnut entered Harvard for a business degree. He passed in 2016, among the last of World War II's POW generation.

The third POW was Corporal August DiPaolo, twenty-four, signal corps of the U.S. Army Air Corps, who also suffered in the Bataan Death March after enlisting in February 1941 and being sent to the Philippines. Born in Buffalo on October 17, 1918, in the Fillmore District and Sidney-Humboldt area, DiPaolo attended School 59 and East High School, working for his father, who was a contractor, until he enlisted on February 2, 1942. He survived the POW camp and died in 2012.

And then there were those who seemed to live a charmed life.

Private First Class Leonard J. "Smiley" Godzich grew up on the East Side on Woltz Avenue and enlisted on his eighteenth birthday. In May 1944, he was assigned to the Ninety-Fourth Infantry and was assigned to Bergholtz, Germany, where he saw Hitler's residence where Adolf Hitler and his mistress Eva Braun lived. Godzich was awarded six medals, including the Bronze Star. He was honorably discharged in 1945 after the war ended and returned home to Buffalo. The Bronze Star Medal is awarded to any person who, after December 6, 1941, while serving in any capacity with the armed forces of the United States, "distinguishes himself or herself by heroic or meritorious achievement or service, not involving participation in aerial flight."

Mr. and Mrs. Edward J. Mallon of Buffalo worried about two sons who enlisted in the service. John R. Mallon, apprentice metalsmith, second class, was in the U.S. Navy in the naval battles of Bismarck and Coral Sea. He was on the cruiser *Chicago*, and when the Japanese sank it in the Solomon Islands, his parents feared that he had perished. Fortunately, he was rescued at sea. Master Sergeant Edward J. Mallon Jr. was with the ADG (Air Depot Group) American Ordnance outfit in England. ADGs provided supplies and repairs. He volunteered for the U.S. Air Borne Glider Infantry, a dangerous option. Mallon wrote his parents and wife that he was convalescing at a base hospital in France. They had feared he was dead.

Three famous heroes of the war had Buffalo connections: William "Wild Bill" Donovan, Robert Jackson and Matt Urban. William Donovan was born in Buffalo, New York, on January 1, 1883. He graduated from Niagara University in 1903, Columbia College in 1905 and Columbia University Law School in 1908. During World War I, Donovan organized and led a battalion of the U.S. Army, the Sixty-Ninth New York Volunteers (known as the "Fighting Sixty-Ninth"). In World War I, he earned the nickname "Wild Bill" for his strong leadership skills and earned the Medal of Honor. As of this writing, he is the only American to have received our nation's four highest awards: the Medal of Honor, the Distinguished Service Cross, the Distinguished Service Medal and the National Security Medal.

After World War I, Donovan returned to Buffalo to practice law. During World War II, he founded, and then led, the Office of Strategic Services, which led to the formation of the Central Intelligence Agency (CIA). After World War II, he served as an assistant to Robert Jackson, chief American prosecutor at the Nuremberg War Crimes Trials. Jackson also had a western New York connection. Although he was born in Pennsylvania, Jackson went to high school in Jamestown and practiced law in Buffalo. President Roosevelt nominated Jackson to the U.S. Supreme Court in 1941.

Matt Urban was born in the Polonia section of Buffalo and attended Cornell University in 1937. Both of his brothers were at the University of Buffalo. As he was in the Reserve Officers' Training Corps (ROTC), he was commissioned a second lieutenant in the army and inducted at Plattsburg, New York, then sent to Fort Bragg, North Carolina, for boot camp and assigned to Company D, Sixtieth Infantry Regiment, Ninth Division, and became a platoon leader and morale officer. He was on a weekend pass on a date when he heard of Pearl Harbor on the radio. For many years, Audie Murphy had been thought to be the most decorated serviceman, with seventy-four awards. But Urban's application was lost and had to be reconstructed years later (1980); he has assumed that title with seventy-seven awards. The Medal of Honor was awarded to him for heroic actions between June and September 1944 in Europe. Erie County erected a statue of Urban in the plaza of the Rath Building. The old state building named after him has been torn down.

Other Buffalonians turned to helping victims of the Holocaust. One German Jew went to great lengths to reach Buffalo and freedom. On January 31, 1939, thirty-five-year-old Isadore Celnik crossed the Niagara River in a rowboat with Edwin Clarence Wagner, forty-two, of Fort Erie, Ontario. Celnik told immigration authorities at Buffalo of being subjected to severe beatings and other mistreatments while a prisoner in a concentration camp for Jews in Germany. Both men were arraigned before U.S. Commissioner Harry E. Harding and committed to jail pending a hearing. Celnik was charged with entering the United States illegally. Immigration order patrolmen arrested the pair at the foot of Ferry Street as the boat pulled into the dock. Celnik said he had been paroled from the camp and given permission to go to Canada for six months. The six months was up last week, and he was trying to reach relatives in Brooklyn Heights. When asked if he wanted to return to Germany, he said, "I will cut my throat first." Attorneys Gordon Gannon and Isadore Raniovitz volunteered their services to prevent Celnik's deportation to Germany and arranged with the prisoner's cousin in New York City to provide him with a bond.

Israel Gaynor Jacobson was the oldest of seven children of Latvian parents. His father was a watchman in a defense plant. He attended Angola High School, then Columbia University, State Teachers College and the University of Buffalo. At the University of Buffalo, he studied social work and completed his master's in 1941. All five of his brothers were in the armed forces during World War II. Jacobson applied for jobs in the FBI and was eager to serve as a social worker in defense positions. The shortage of social workers during the 1940s encouraged social work schools like the University of Buffalo to provide accelerated programs. Jacobson supported himself by supervising recreational programs for Jewish social agencies in Rochester.

Niles Carpenter, the dean of social work at the University of Buffalo, was genuinely fond of Jacobson and corresponded with him. In October 1944, Jacobson visited Italy as a member of the American Jewish Joint Distribution Committee (aka "The Joint") to aid in refugee work. He wrote to Carpenter in September 1945 to describe the tragic situation in Greece: "90 percent of Greek Jews deported by Greeks and Bulgarians, 90 percent perished in camps, and 60 children in an overcrowded orphanage." Jacobson wrote to his mentor "because of wide experience here and in Italy I have decided not to return to Rochester." He began to direct "Joint" activities for Jewish refugees. In 1944, he was handpicked by the organization to supervise postwar reconstruction activities for Jewish refugees in Greece, Portugal, North Africa, Hungary, Czechoslovakia and Italy. In late 1944, he was arrested and detained for several weeks by the Hungarian police. His wife was also a social worker and student of Dr. Jacobson. By 1961, Carpenter had been appointed director of the Latin American headquarters of the United Hebrew International Aid Society (HIAS), and several years later, he became the executive vice president of HIAS.

Air raid warden Celia Slohm (Bernstein), a Buffalo resident, was elected national president of Junior Hadassah in 1933. Under her guidance, the organization worked with a cooperative children's village near Haifa in Palestine. Thousands of German refugee children between eight and fourteen were brought to the country by the Bureau for the Settlement of Refugee Children in Palestine, and 10 were placed with a village of 110 boys and girls. Hadassah, the Women's Zionist Organization of America, is an American Jewish volunteer women's organization founded in 1912. (Palestine was under British mandate until 1948, when Israel was declared a state.)

The Buffalo Jewish community welcomed three hundred Holocaust survivors, refugees from Europe, and helped them settle into the area. The quota set by the U.S. Department of State was low, so some traveled from Canada, Israel, China or South America to Buffalo.

Max Schmeidler was a Jewish refugee who ended up in Shanghai, China, where he served as a policeman, eventually working his way to the United States. An estimated seventeen thousand German and Austrian Jews came to Shanghai after the beginning of Nazi persecution of Jews. The community could not support so many newcomers and turned to the Joint Distribution Committee in New York for additional funding. Schmeidler contracted polio in China as a young man and came to Buffalo in 1946 where he started a family.

By the late 1950s, most of the Jewish refugees headed for Buffalo had started a new life in western New York. My friends and I attended public school with children of Holocaust survivors and never knew it.

9

VICTORY

JAPS QUIT
JAP SURRENDER COMPLETE
NATION IN JOYOUS FRENZY AT NEWS
BUFFALO GOES WILD; THOUSANDS DOWNTOWN

The *Courier Express* headlines of Wednesday, August 15, 1945, aptly described the delirious happiness of the crowd of 100,000 in the pouring rain the previous evening. Drivers honked and slowed down as Buffalonians cried, screamed and blew horns and whistles. They banged on drums, improvised or not, and threw streamers, paper strips, bits of cloth and ticker tape from upper windows. The bars were full, and people of all ages waved miniature American flags. Church bells rang in thanksgiving. Souvenir hunters tore apart a papier-mâché reproduction of the Liberty Bell used by the J.N. Adam store for war bond drives.

At Main and Court, a group of girls climbed onto a jeep driven by two military policemen and smothered them with kisses, wrote reporter Joseph Slotkin.

Betty Goulding, nineteen, of Dunkirk was a student nurse at Children's Hospital. "My sister is a nurse in the U.S. Army. She's been overseas two years and is only 21. I'm glad I didn't have to see the sights she did."

Army sergeant Louis Tubolino, thirty-four, was thrilled that he wouldn't have to worry about his brother, Joseph, twenty-four, who was an ordnance sergeant in the Pacific. "Joe got the Purple Heart. I was only in the supply

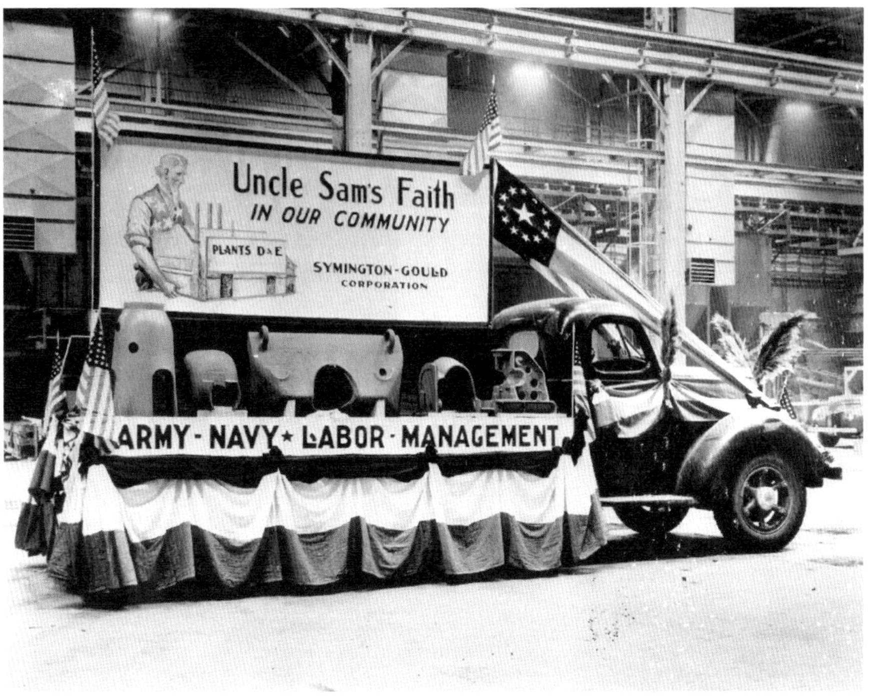

Patriotic parade in the Tonawandas. *Courtesy of the Historical Society of the Tonawandas.*

lines of Russia and Iran for 29 months. Brother, stay out of Iran if you want a vacation. And those Russians are rugged in all ways."

Following President Truman's order for a two-day holiday for all federal employees, the mayor declared that city employees also be given two days off. For three days, the city celebrated as offices and plants remained closed. Canisius High School and College, and State Teachers weren't open, but the University of Buffalo resumed summer classes. At one hundred by sixty feet, the third-largest flag in the nation was draped across the front of the J.N. Adams store. On either side of Old Glory were the colors of eighteen Allied nations. Banks were scheduled to reopen, but the only post office service available was a window for stamp sales at Swan and Ellicott Streets.

The *Buffalo Evening News* and its sister radio station WBEN sponsored a victory celebration in Delaware Park with radio celebrity Clint Buehlman as the master of ceremonies. Fireworks, tributes to the war dead, the mayor's recitation of war production statistics and "God Bless America" sung by the crowd of 110,000 stirred hearts. After the national anthem was sung, the crowd, row upon row, struck matches to shed light like the stars above upon the meadow. Three boys carried around a hanging effigy of Japanese Emperor Hirohito. The "awful cost of victory—10,000 Buffalo and Western New York casualties" said the mayor in an official proclamation. (Note, this estimate was high.)

On the South Side, the Tri-Abbott–South Park Businessmen's Association sponsored an outing at Crystal Beach. The ban on gasoline was finally lifted. Most visitors came to see the games in the beach stadium, including the fifty-yard dash, the hoop contest, nail-driving, pie-eating and egg-tossing.

Along the Riverside section, impromptu parades and American flags moved down Tonawanda Street. Children, with help from their parents, placed red, white and blue streamers on the top of light poles. On Ontario Street, in the Riverside Theatre, an employee announced the Japanese surrender, and many patrons left to celebrate. At Military and Skillin, a ticker tape parade began to shower motorists with bits of paper and confetti.

On the West Side, car horns blasted as teenagers drove down Busti Avenue and Niagara Street. Their parents, who were glad to have a holiday from defense work, talked of their sons and others in service, wondering when they would return. Veterans spoke of their relief and happiness at being home for good.

The Fort Niagara veterans' celebration was "mild," but what they really wanted to know was when they would be discharged. The commanding officer allowed the German POWs to hear the victory news over the radio.

In Lackawanna, residents marched down Ridge Road cheering and singing. Our Lady of Victory Basilica conducted special services every hour during the day and in the evening. Large crowds danced and cheered on Walden Avenue and Genesee Street and along William Street and Delavan Avenue in Cheektowaga. And in the Tonawandas, a giant victory parade led by the Legion Post and Gratwick Hose Company was followed by joyful residents "in the wildest celebration the cities ever witnessed." Kenmore, Williamsville and Amherst citizens drove or took public transportation into Buffalo to celebrate.

Phone girls cleared lines for servicemen's calls. The calls from debarkation points on the East and West Coasts were spotted. The operators tipped one another off with "this is a service call." The operator asked parties in the busy local line to hold for the service call. Most soldiers called between 7:00 p.m. and 10:00 p.m. so that they could catch their fathers home from the office. The phone lines were jammed for four days.

When the holiday was over, thousands stood in long lines for jobless benefits. They had been released from defense jobs and were now eligible for unemployment benefits. More women than men waited for their applications to be processed at the 174th Regiment Armory at Niagara and Connecticut Streets. The benefits could reach twenty-one dollars per week for up to twenty-six weeks if needed. Many of the women workers said they weren't planning to return to work after their unemployment benefits ended. Several women were inspectors at Colonial Radio.

"They told us they'd call us when we are needed," said a former employee. "I suppose I'll go back to work if they do, but I know that a lot of my friends won't."

"War contract cancellations may cause between 45,000 to 50,000 unemployed," stated the federal government's representative, Joseph Canty. He explained that most defense plants would reduce their hours from forty-eight to forty per week, which would require more workers to be added. Over one-third of the jobless would leave the labor force due to retirement or disinterest. Defense workers would return to retail and trade jobs (now filled by high school dropouts or essential employees), and "quite a few" war plant workers would return to agriculture.

But war contracts were terminated more severely and quickly than Canty expected. The navy canceled contracts with twenty-one firms in western New York. Curtiss-Wright announced that its Buffalo and Kenmore plants would be closed temporarily. The Bell Aircraft plant announced the possible purchase of the Niagara Falls plant from the federal government. The Elmwood Plant was converted into storage space for surplus manufacturing equipment.

But the light industry jobs at Curtiss-Wright ended for good when the company, which had lost its wartime contracts, left Buffalo and concentrated its efforts on the Columbus, Ohio plant. Several years later, the company assets were sold, and Curtiss-Wright was only a memory.

Homefront families had yet another fear for their children when a polio epidemic in 1944 delayed opening of schools and daycare centers for months after a four-year-old child from Eden was admitted to the hospital. Soon after, more children from Eden displayed symptoms. By mid-June, the polio scare had been declared an epidemic, and by August, the weekly hospital admission rate had climbed to eighty patients. Previous polio epidemics in 1916 and 1939 had sensitized residents to the horror of infantile paralysis. (The Salk vaccine was not available until 1961.) This time, over nineteen thousand polio cases ravaged the United States. Erie County had over one thousand cases, but Niagara Falls was spared. Between May and September 1944, seven hundred patients were admitted to Children's Hospital, which had been converted to treat polio victims only. The disease struck children, teenagers and young adults in their twenties. Family members were threatened with lengthy separations, worries about possible disabilities, and financial hardship. Most of all, they feared the worst. The hospital made an annex into a ward of iron lungs, but those were a temporary help. Funerals were small. A nurse who had treated polio patients at Children's would not be interviewed due to the painful memories she had of that time.

No one knew how the virus spread. The public health department banned public funerals for fear of contagion; ordered that school openings be delayed one month; and closed playgrounds, swimming pools, nursery schools and daycare centers. Routine operations such as tonsil and adenoid operations scheduled for children were canceled, as the officials feared links between surgery and the disease. Parents kept children at home and forbade them to attend movie theaters or play team sports.

County fairs, summer fetes, parades and picnics were canceled. Some families left town or sent their children away to reside with distant relatives until the epidemic subsided in mid-December. When the worst of the epidemic was over, the state had a new problem: disabled children and young adults who needed special services. Fortunately, less than 1 percent of cases ended in paralysis. Decades later, researchers discovered that the virus was spread by fecal or oral routes and affected the nervous system. Fortunately, since 1991, there have been no cases of polio in the Western Hemisphere since widespread vaccination.

Historian Richard Rhodes stated that Japan, although losing the war, its people subsisting on one thousand calories or fewer daily, likely held out for a conditional surrender. After Roosevelt died during his fourth term as president, President Harry S Truman—although kept out of the loop about the atomic bomb's development—made the decision to drop bombs on two Japanese cities. On August 6, the B-29 *Enola Gay* dropped the uranium bomb of thirteen kilotons on Hiroshima. "Little Boy," as the bomb was nicknamed, killed up to 200,000 people.

On August 9, the second bomb, known as "Fat Man," was dropped on Nagasaki, its secondary target, killing eighty thousand. On August 15, the Japanese informally surrendered. That was the news Americans had been waiting for—the true end of the war, victory over Japan (V-J Day). Nineteen Buffalonians witnessed the formal unconditional surrender of Japan on the USS *Missouri* on September 2, 1945, in Tokyo Bay.

Western New York participated in creating the bombs. Buffalonians were part of the Manhattan Project. Captain B.G. Seitz, a graduate of Fosdick-

Masten Parks High School and the Rensselaer Polytechnic Institute, was a civil engineer in the U.S. Army Corps of Engineers. He was a statistics officer at Clinton Engineering Works at Oak Ridge, Tennessee.

Lawrence Riordan, who graduated from St. Bonaventure University in 1935, was with the Manhattan Project from the beginning before employment at Dupont on River Road in Tonawanda.

Jack W. Zuidema of Lockport graduated from Hobart College, worked at Eastern Kodak in Rochester and transferred to Oak Ridge in 1943. He returned to western New York.

Alfred Brooks Jr., a resident of Wellsville, also graduated in 1943 from Hobart College and worked for the Lake Ontario Ordnance Works in Niagara County and Columbia University's War Research Board. The ordnance works covered 7,500 acres just north of Niagara Falls.

Robert Dahler of Buffalo attended Bennett High School and graduated from the University of Rochester. He worked for the Linde Air Products Company and the Lake Ontario Ordnance Works before joining the War Research Bureau. The bureau sent him to work as a chemical engineer to research the atomic bomb for two years before he became a process supervisor at Oak Ridge.

Marcelles "Marc" Lee Weidenbeck of Bowmansville graduated from Canisius College in 1941 and earned a PhD in physics at the University of Notre Dame. During the war, he presented a scientific paper on cosmic rays before the Buffalo Society of Natural Science. Major W.O. Swanson from Jamestown coordinated the group.

Buffalo native Jean Burke Fancourt graduated from the Buffalo Seminary and Mt. Holyoke College with a degree in chemistry. Her first job was at Hewitt Rubber working on the development of synthetic rubber. In 1944, she joined Hooker Chemical as an analytical chemist and was completely unaware she had participated in secret research for the Manhattan Project until she received a certificate of commendation in the mail. Afterward, Fancourt worked in the Erie County Clerk's Office.

Should America have used the bomb? Using the new weapon was cheaper, the public was told, than an invasion of Japan. The bombs cost $2 billion ($27 trillion in 2016 dollars). The army retained seven million men because the number of eighteen-year-olds was insufficient to meet induction enlistments. Large numbers of seventeen-year-old enlistments left the Selective Service no choice but to draft men aged eighteen to thirty who had been deferred to their skilled employment in defense industries.

In Buffalo, the newly formed Civic Full Employment Committee warned that the new weapon would put defense plants out of work. The committee cautioned the city and county that thirteen thousand former war workers would double to twenty-sex thousand. The back-to-school movement begun in 1944 moved in to high gear to encourage hundreds of high school dropouts to resume their education, else they would glut the market now and remain unskilled later.

The economy began—slowly—to transition into a postwar world. Politicians promised full employment. Low-interest loans at less than 1 percent from commercial banks financed 70 percent of World War II and postwar reconstruction. Establishing exclusive trade agreements with Latin America for raw materials and with Saudi Arabia for oil helped the federal government pay debts.

Petroleum was crucial to the war effort. Over 90 percent of the seven billion barrels of oil used in the war came from the United States, which produced 63 percent of the world's oil and supplied the Allies. In 1940, only 5 percent of the world's oil came from the Middle East. Because America's domestic supply was dwindling, Roosevelt instructed a wartime agency to appraise the oil potential of Saudi Arabia and its neighbors. "The oil in this region is the greatest single prize in all of history," reported a staffer. By 1943, Roosevelt had authorized direct financial aid to Saudi Arabia. But for last-minute opposition from the American oil industry, the president nearly established a U.S. government–owned oil company in Saudi Arabia after striking a bargain with Texaco. By 1948, when Germany and Japan were under occupation, the United States had become dependent on foreign oil.

Higher taxes, forced savings, frugality, full employment, rationing, price ceilings and wage freezes coupled with federal borrowing paid for World War II and postwar reconstruction. Would those measures work today? More to the point, would Americans emulate the "Greatest Generation" in sacrifice and service to the nation?

10

POSTWAR BLUES

In mid-1944, plants laid off thousands of men and women as war contracts from the army and navy were cancelled. The last hired were the first fired. Men began to return from the battleground, paying their own way after being demobilized at Sampson Naval Training Station near Seneca Lake or through other large military facilities. Sampson could handle eight hundred servicemen daily. But home wasn't always what they expected.

Many vets were under the impression that everyone on the homefront was making $100 a week in a soft job. But it was $0.75 and $0.85 an hour at hard work, long hours, stiff taxes and job insecurity that changed their minds.

Radio operator John Pruzinsky commented, "Gosh, all we did was talk about how we'd spend all the soft money we'd make when we got home. I was disappointed when I found out how things really were!"

Early returnees had the best of both worlds, if their health was good. After one and a half years of service, Private First Class Paul Zahm returned to Buffalo in mid-1942 to his old job as a crane operator at a steel plant. "I've always wanted to be a chemist," he said, "and with the GI Bill and my savings from war work, I'll be able to swing it."

"I don't think I'll find my way back to my old line of work," said his buddy. "Besides, I'd always wanted to get into business administration. Right now, I'm trying for a civil service job. I'll work days and go to school nights."

Veterans brought home souvenirs from the war, Japanese flags, handguns and Japanese invasion money, hastily printed as scrip by Japan, and worthless.

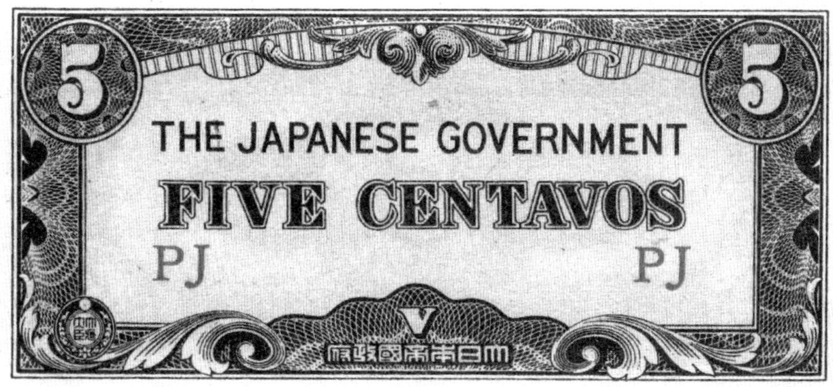

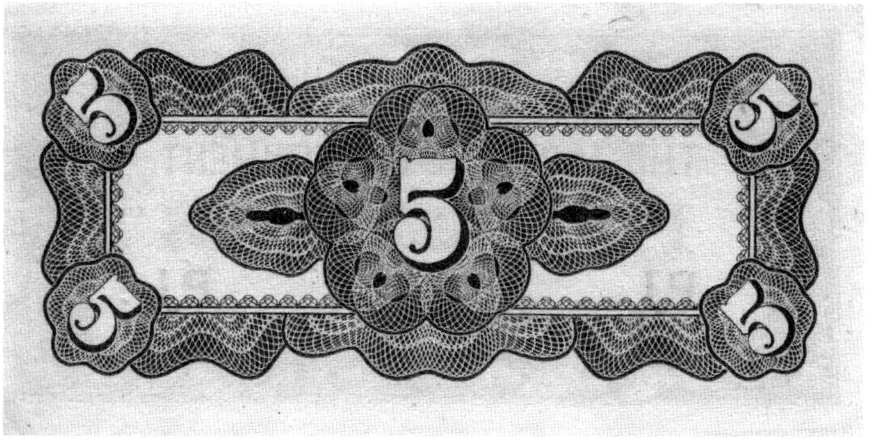

Worthless Japanese invasion currency, known as scrip or "Mickey Mouse money." *Author's collection.*

Black market prices and rationing points angered returning servicemen. In a few cases, the family dog had received a ration book because Grandpa signed him up as a dependent.

Jack Sprat can eat no fat
His wife can eat no lean
Meat shortage and black markets
Keep their platter clean.

By Joseph Roche

Jobs were hard to find. Servicemen wore demobilization badges ("the ruptured duck") when they were in civilian clothes to remind prospective employers they were veterans, but so did most of the other unemployed. The first Selective Service Act had promised that their jobs would be held for them for one year of service. That was no longer true. The no-strike rule was gone. Bell Aircraft's 1949 strike would go down in the history books. But other jobs for semi-skilled or skilled tradesmen became available, sufficient to live the American Dream of a house and family. The baby boom produced a need for schools and teachers. The center of commerce moved away from downtown to the suburbs. Universities and colleges provided—and still do—educational opportunities. But there's one side effect of the war that just won't go away.

Western New York's connection to the creation of the atomic bomb has become more troubling in the last forty years. Although no one thought this revelation was a secret, in February 1981, the *New York Times* reported that the army and defense contractors buried over thirty-seven million gallons of radioactive caustic wastes between 1944 and 1946 in the town of Tonawanda, particularly the 14150 zip code. My zip code. In the 1960s, well before the Clean Air and Water Acts, we all knew that Lake Erie's sludge was harmful, and it was the punchline of jokes on late-night talk shows. Swimming or water skiing in the Niagara River was not encouraged. Anyone who lived or worked in Niagara Falls smelled the plumes of pollution from Hooker and Union Carbide and the rows of chemical plants along the Robert Moses Parkway.

When the south wind blew in the 1930s and '40s, the city of Buffalo's drinking water became contaminated from phenol, a runoff from industry. Phenol is a lethal chemical. The Nazis used its vapors or the injection of one gram in Jews to kill them.

In January 1941, the War Department acted quickly to acquire ten thousand acres in Niagara County to build a huge munitions plant, later called the Lake Ontario Ordnance Works (LOOW), to manufacture TNT. The plant's location, a mile east of the Niagara River and north of Niagara Falls, beat out Rochester, which was considered too far away from the chemicals, personnel, electrical power and railroad access needed. The residents, aware of months of secret surveys of the area, were convinced that a new military airport was the real purpose. But the military revealed that the plant needed thirty million gallons of water daily and proximity to Fort Niagara for security. Everything about the project was secret, and the military ordered farmers to leave their lands immediately. Residents protested to their congressmen. The Niagara Frontier Planning Board argued that seven thousand of the acres selected were among the most fertile land in the state and the rest had "some of the best suburban homes and estates" in western New York. Others complained that removing ten thousand acres from the tax rolls would raise property taxes for the remaining county residents. The board suggested to the military that the plant be moved to Pendleton, Cambria or Wheatfield, but the military told them that "patriotic considerations must outweigh all others." In the end, there was nothing the inhabitants could do. They were given thirty days to move, and their houses were taken down. The munitions plant was built in haste by 7,500 workers.

The LOOW also was more than a TNT plant. As noted after the Nagasaki bomb drop, forty western New York plants helped develop the bomb, and several thousand metallurgists, chemists and war workers were employed over the war's last two and a half years in "the best-kept secret of the war." No one knew the end use to which the products they created were to be put. A special plant was constructed at the Linde Air Products ceramic plant on East Park Drive and Woodward Avenue in the town of Tonawanda. The National Carbon Company, the Electro Metallurgical Company and the Hooker Electrochemical Company in the Niagara Falls area contributed significantly. (Linde, National Carbon and Electro Metallurgical were subsidiaries of the Union Carbide Corporation.) Other plants include Buffalo Bolt Company in North Tonawanda, Buffalo Foundry, Buffalo Meter, Farrar and Trefts, Allegheny Ludlum Steel and Wiesner-Rapp. Over thirty other Buffalo-area companies provided machines, tools and equipment for the project. At one time, every tool and die plant and every machine shop in Buffalo was turning out something for this project. Union Carbide had hinted that the company and its subsidiaries would work with the federal government on the atomic bomb to "assure a lasting peace."

In the 1950s and '60s, one of the buildings was used as a boron-10 isotope separation plant. The employees were not given protection against radiation. All the contaminated materials stored at the former LOOW site—such as thorium, uranium and the world's largest concentration of radiuim-226—are buried in a ten-acre storage site. The plutonium-injected animals from the University of Rochester are buried at the LOOW site, as is television broadcaster Tom Brokaw's anthrax-exposed desk, because that was the only disposal site that could handle it.

Returning to the *Times* article, most western New Yorkers thought that the contractors (and army) had no business dumping residue "from the atomic bomb project's centers around the country" on the ground and in makeshift buildings. Workers were exposed to "excessive levels of radiation." Linde's ceramics plant mentioned earlier was a secret plant for uranium ore processing. The ore came from northwest of Ottawa, Ontario. In 1979, officials identified properties—personal and commercial—contaminated with radioactive industrial waste. Some were pavement (slag) stone. Forty years ago, house pavements in Lewiston and Niagara Falls were known to have radiation levels seventy times than what's found in the natural environment. At least sixty properties in Niagara County and Grand Island where children play and people live are hot spots, and the only remedy is for the material to be cleaned up and removed. It's not easy or cheap. None of these sites qualify for the Superfund program.

The list of sites in Lewiston, Grand Island, Tonawanda and Niagara Falls is staggering, and it's not complete. Property values have fallen in some areas. The worst of the Manhattan Project aftermath is its effect on the workers. In the 1990s, the state health department conducted a study of cancer sites in western New York. They found significant clusters for thyroid, breast, prostate and lung cancers—far beyond the average for the nation. The second study retracted the findings and stated that the difference was only 10 percent for all cancers, which could be accounted for by smoking.

In 1991, Manhattan Project radioactive wastes were discovered in the fifty-five-acre Tonawanda landfill. The Riverview Elementary School is near the site. Four other sites are being monitored as of 2015: one in Lockport, one (Linde Air/Praxair) in Tonawanda, one in Niagara Falls and a second Tonawanda landfill.

In 2016 a ten-year public health study began to determine how the Tonawanda Coke's operations on River Road in the town of Tonawanda affected residents.

Most of the LOOW site has been sold off and put to civilian use. The Basilica Shrine of Our Lady of Fatima is built on part of the site. It's the only Catholic church that has a mural with an atomic bomb mushroom cloud behind the altar. And now I know why.

EPILOGUE

Unlike World War I, the war never had its own holiday. World War II ended on two different dates: V-E Day in Europe was May 8, 1945, and V-J Day in the Pacific was August 14, 1945. The official surrender of the Japanese government was September 2, 1945. The war dead of Pearl Harbor were not memorialized until 1962, when the underwater graves of those in the USS *Arizona* were left on the harbor floor.

Although President Truman encouraged citizens to observe V-J as "Victory Day," Americans remember the dead of both world wars on Veterans' Day (formerly Armistice Day) on November 11.

Memorial Day, established for the memory of those fallen during the Civil War, has been expanded to include all veterans who died in active military service. This holiday, which marks the unofficial start of summer, is observed on the last Monday in May.

As in most cities in America, memorials of stone, streets and the names of VFW and American Legion posts abounded in the early years after the war. Many are bronze plaques in hallways of public buildings or schools. Others, like the South Park High School historic marker (1946, restored 1999), are made of stone surrounded by a small garden. In Cheektowaga are three memorials to the same fallen hero, Leonard J. Post Jr. Near the Walden Galleria is a small street and standing memorial at the street's entrance dedicated to him. And a mile west on Walden Avenue is the Leonard J. Post Jr. Post No. 6251, aka the Leonard Post. The building of the Walden Galleria forced relocation from the original site established in 1948. This was my father's post. He was a proud life member. To paraphrase from the post's history,

> *Leonard Post Jr. was one of the first men in the Walden neighborhood to sacrifice his life in World War II. He was inducted into the army on February 25, 1943. On June 12 ,1944, six days after the invasion began, he was wounded in Normandy, France. Two days later, he died at the age of twenty and was buried in the U.S. Military Cemetery at St. Laurent, France. His remains were repatriated in 1947.*

The exact number of servicemen and women who died in World War II, whether killed in action, died of wounds later, died of starvation in POW camps, killed in noncombat conditions (e.g, car accident, heart attack stateside) or missing in action and presumed dead, will never be known. The World War II honor roll prepared by the *Buffalo News* (1947) and the World War II deaths by county and city in the New York State Military Museum (1946), despite the official volumes used for the museum, and the meticulous work of volunteers, are erroneous. The official records state that 405,399 lost their lives in the war (including 78,976 missing in action), with 233,131 returned for burial. An additional 93,242 veterans were buried at American Battle Monuments Commission cemeteries in Europe in sixteen foreign countries although three cemeteries remain in the United States. (e.g., Honolulu Memorial).

The Buffalo and Erie County Naval and Military Park was established in 1979 as the Buffalo Naval and Servicemen's Park and is the largest inland naval park in the nation. The popular lakeside museum in Canalside is home to the destroyer USS *The Sullivans*, the cruiser USS *Little Rock* and the submarine USS *Croaker*, which are open to the public.

The USS *Croaker* is one of seventeen submarines that survived the war. It was brought to Buffalo in 1988 and, after repairs, welcomed visitors in 1989. The USS *Little Rock*, a cruiser launched in 1944, was open to visitors ten years earlier. Among its grounds are memorials to service personnel from different armed forces and wars. Other naval vessels, aircraft and vehicles allow for visitor inspection. The Wall of Honor displays memorial bricks with the names of veterans. The USS *The Sullivans* destroyer has great significance to many older veterans and to my family personally.

The Sullivans were five brothers from Waterloo, Iowa, who all joined the navy and were assigned to the same ship, the USS *Juneau*, a cruiser. On November 13, 1942, during the Battle of Guadalcanal, a Japanese torpedo

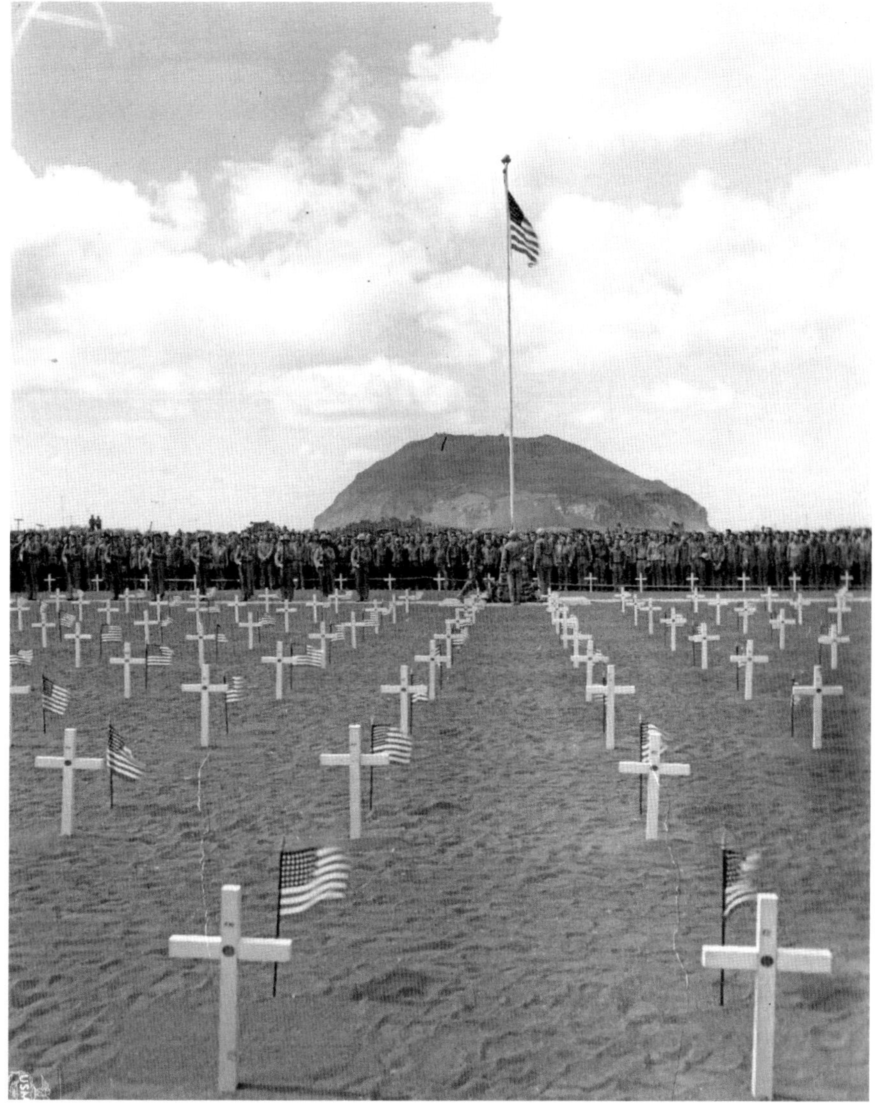

Fifth Marine Division cemetery, Iwo Jima. *Courtesy of the Buffalo History Museum, used by permission.*

destroyed the ship. Albert, Madison, Francis and Joseph died immediately. George was one of about one hundred men floating in the water, clinging to parts of the ship. He managed to secure a life raft but did not survive due to exposure to the elements or menacing sharks. Only ten of the seven hundred men aboard ship survived. Mr. and Mrs. Sullivan received word that their boys were missing in action but would not know of their deaths until June 1942.

My father was assigned to the USS *Juneau*. At the last minute, he was sent to aircraft mechanic school in Jacksonville. Would he have survived or gone down with the Sullivan brothers?

Many years ago, I saw a 1944 movie called *The Fighting Sullivans* about the tragedy. At the end, the five brothers are depicted as ghostly forms smiling in the sky. In western New York, a paranormal organization believes that George haunts the USS *The Sullivans*, searching for his brothers. Due to the tragedy, a 1948 directive was added. To date, the Department of Defense maintains the Sole Survivor Policy to protect son(s) (and later, daughters) from the draft or combat duty who had a combat-related death in the family.

In 2010, Lisa Wylie and her sister Jo-Anne established Honor Flight Buffalo, which has flown five hundred World War II veterans to Washington, D.C., to visit the World War II Memorial, Vietnam Memorial and Arlington National Cemetery. The original organization was disbanded due to the volunteers' time commitments, and Buffalo Niagara Honor Flight has continued the experience of a lifetime. The trip takes veterans from World War II, Korea and Vietnam free of charge with their family members. Similar associations exist across the nation, bringing back memories, sad and sweet, to veterans.

Dedicated in 2004, the World War II Memorial in Washington, D.C., honors the 16 million who served in the armed forces of the United States, the more than 400,000 who died and all who supported the war effort on the homefront.

The most recent memorial for war heroes is the Circle of Heroes military monument in the Buffalo and Erie County Naval and Military Park in Canalside established in summer 2017. Among those honored with a bronze statue will be Medal of Honor winners Lieutenant Colonel Matt Urban, the most decorated soldier of World War II; William "Wild Bill" Donovan, "Father of the Central Intelligence Agency"; and Gunnery Sergeant John "Manila" F. Basilone. Donovan is the only person to have received all four of the United States' highest awards. Navy Cross winner Lieutenant Commander C. Wade McClusky Jr., hero of the Battle of Midway, will also be represented. My hope is that Buffalo-born Major General Carroll W. McColpin, commanding officer of the 404th Fighter Bomber Group, will be included because of his service with the Eagle Squadron in 280 combat missions.

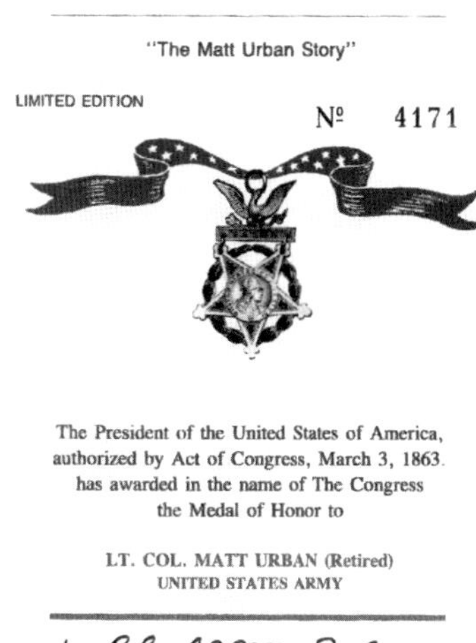

Matt Urban's book plate and signature. *Author's collection.*

The United States Holocaust Memorial Museum was established in 1993 as the United States' official memorial to the Holocaust for the documentation, study and interpretation of Holocaust history. Ten years earlier, the Holocaust Resource Center of Buffalo was created. Its mission is to "Teach the Lessons of the Holocaust, Remember the Events of the Holocaust and Honor the Survivors and Victims of the Holocaust." This living reminder of the worst genocide in the twentieth century educates the public, teachers and students through survivor testimonies and workshops. We must never forget.

According to Buffalo historian Mark Goldman, "The war was good for Buffalo. It was the best thing, in fact, that had ever happened to the city, and everybody tried to get into it." Oral historian Studs Terkel stated that World War II was "a good war." World War II historian Michael Adams said that the "good war" was violent, vicious and horrific. Michael Kilian commented in the *Buffalo News*, "The Good War, a global slaughter that took the lives of some 50 million people, had its bad side." And so it did: alliance with Josef Stalin, leader of the USSR, as murderous as Hitler, allowed occupation of half of Europe by the Communists. Between 110,000 and 120,000 Japanese Americans were forcibly removed to live in camps around the United States.

And the good side? World War II catalyzed the social and economic development of the middle class, giving blue-collar workers the opportunity to live the American Dream. Of the 16 million men and women in the armed services, 418,520 paid the final price. (In comparison, 620,000 men died in the American Civil War.) The Serviceman's Readjustment Act of 1944, also known as the G.I. Bill, provided $33 billion in low-interest mortgages, gave 9 million veterans opportunities to attend college or specialized training and expanded the number of federal hospitals for veterans. Historians credit the bill for jumpstarting a period of prosperity that lasted until the 1970s.

In 2012, Louis R. Palma, director of Erie County's Veterans' Service, told a *Buffalo News* reporter, "Ten years from now, when most of us are gone, there won't be anyone with first-hand experience to talk about the war anymore." A Leonard J. Post VFW member confided to me, "Some veterans, though, don't want to tell their stories to anyone."

As my mother, defense worker and war bride, wrote of my father: "To him and many many others, this was important at that time in his life. There was no great fanfare when he left, and there was none when he returned. And this is the way it was for most of 'the boys.' We were very mindful that so many did not make it home. It was a different time."

BIBLIOGRAPHY

Abels, Margaret. "Western New York Women in Defense Industries, World War II." Western New York Heritage Institute, Canisius College. Unpublished manuscript, 1989.

Adams, Leonard P. *Wartime Manpower Mobilization: A Study of the World War II Experience in the Buffalo-Niagara Area.* Ithaca, NY: Cornell University, 1951.

Adams, Michael. *The Best War Ever: America and World War II.* Baltimore, MD: Johns Hopkins University, 1994.

Aquila, Richard. *Home Front Soldier: The Story of a GI and His Italian American Family During World War II.* Albany: State University of New York, 1999.

Astor, Gerald. *Wings of Gold: The U.S. Naval Air Campaign in World War II.* New York: Presidio, 2004.

Dietz, Suzanne S. *Honor Thy Fathers and Mothers: Niagara Frontier's Legacy of Patriotism and Survival.* N.p.: privately published, 2008.

Duling, Gretchen A. *A Legacy of Mutual Trust.* Youngstown, NY: Old Fort Niagara Association, 2009.

Flynn, George Q. *The Draft, 1940–1973.* Lawrence: University Press of Kansas, 1993.

Fried, Emanuel. *Most Dangerous Man.* Kansas City, KS: John Brown Press, 2010.

Fuentes, Nancy. *Two Brothers, One War: As Told Through the Letters of Roman and Edward Baratz.* Buffalo, NY: NFB, 2015.

Gibbs, Lois M. *Love Canal: The Story Continues.* Stoney Creek, CT: New Society, 1998.

Goldman, Mark. *City on the Edge: Buffalo, New York*. Amherst, NY: Prometheus, 2007.

———. *High Hopes: The Rise and Decline of Buffalo, NY.* Albany: State University of New York, 1983.

Hartzell, Karl. *The Empire State at War: World War II*. Albany: State of New York, 1949.

Hausauer, Kenneth C. *The Second Fifty Years: A History of the Young Men's Christian Association of Buffalo and Erie County, 1902–1952*. Buffalo, NY: YMCA, 1952.

Hill, Robert A., ed. *The FBI's RACON: Racial Conditions in the United States during World War II*. Boston: Northeastern University Press, 1995.

Iggers, Wilma, and Georg Iggers. *Two Lives in Uncertain Times: Facing the Challenges of the 20th Century as Scholars and Citizens*. New York: Berghahn, 2006.

Kahn, E., ed. *Fighting Divisions: Histories of Each U.S. Combat Division in World War II*. Washington, D.C.: Zenger, 1983.

Kennedy, David M. *Freedom from Fear: The American People in Depression and War, 1929–1945*. New York: Oxford University Press, 2001.

Kington, Donald M. *Forgotten Summers: The Story of the Citizens' Military Training Camps, 1921–1940*. San Francisco: Two Decades, 1995.

Klein, Gerda W. *All but My Life*. 2nd ed. New York: Hill & Yang, 1995.

Klein, Maury. *A Call to Arms: Mobilizing America for World War II*. New York: Bloomsbury, 2014.

Krammer, Arnold. *Nazi Prisoners of War in America*. Lanham, MD: Scarborough, 1996.

Kratts, Michelle A. *Niagara Falls in World War II*. Charleston, SC: The History Press, 2016.

Lingeman, Richard R. *Don't You Know There's a War On?* New York: Capricorn, 1976.

Meyer, Agnes E. *Journey through Chaos*. New York: Harcourt Brace, 1943.

Miller, Nathan. *War at Sea: A Naval History of World War II*. New York: Oxford, 1995.

Neucomb, Richard F. *Iwo Jima*. 2nd ed. New York: First Owl, 2002.

O'Neil, William. *A Democracy at War: America's Fight at Home and Abroad in World War II*. New York: Free Press, 1993.

Ploughman, Penelope. *Love Canal*. Charleston, SC: Arcadia Publishing, 2013.

Rhodes, Richard. *The Making of the Atomic Bomb*. 2nd ed. New York: Simon and Schuster, 2012.

Rizzo, Michael F. *Through the Mayors' Eyes*. Buffalo, NY: Old House History, 2005.

Sides, Hampton. *Ghost Soldiers: The Forgotten Epic Story of World War II's Most Dramatic Mission.* New York: Doubleday, 2001.

Silsby, Robert W. *Settlement to Suburb: A History of the Town of Tonawanda, Erie County, New York, 1707–1986.* Tonawanda, NY: Sommer, 1997.

Sunseri, Alvin, and Kenneth Lyftogt. *The Sullivan Family of Waterloo.* Cedar Falls, IA: M&M Publishing, 1998.

Sweeney, Daniel J., ed. *Buffalo and Erie County, 1914–1919.* 2nd ed., Buffalo, NY: Committee of One Hundred, 1920.

Toll, Ian. *The Conquering Tide: War in the Pacific Islands, 1942–1944.* New York: W.W. Norton, 2016.

Tuttle, William. *Daddy's Gone to War: The Second World War in the Lives of America's Children.* New York: Oxford University Press, 1993.

Urban, Matt. *The Matt Urban Story*. Holland, MI: privately published, 1989.

Yellin, Emily. *Our Mothers' War: American Women at Home and at the Front During World War II.* New York: Free Press, 2014.

Yianilos, Theresa Karas. *Woman Marine: A Memoir of a Woman Who Joined the U.S. Marine Corps in World War II to Free a Marine to Fight.* La Jolla, CA: La Jolla Book Publishing, 1994.

INDEX

ABOUT THE AUTHOR

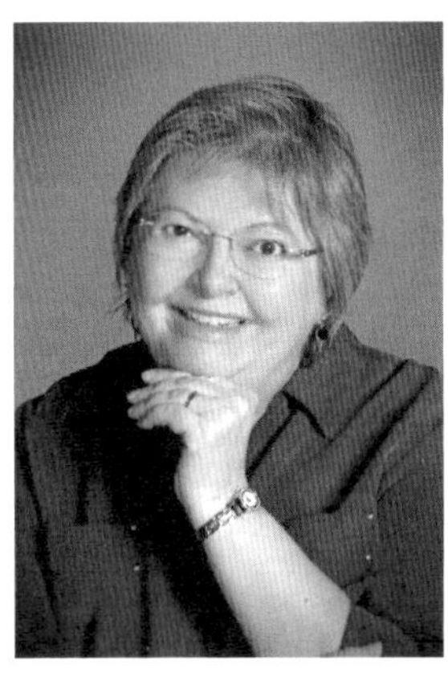

Gretchen Knapp, PhD, is a native of the greater Buffalo area from the town of Tonawanda. She earned her doctorate in history from the University at Buffalo and MLS from the University of Maryland. Knapp taught U.S. history and archives at Illinois State University and received fellowships from the New York State Archives, the University of Minnesota Social Welfare Archives and the Herbert Hoover Presidential Library. She lives in central Illinois with her husband.